THE CONCERN FOR SOCIAL JUSTICE
IN THE
PURITAN REVOLUTION

William Walwyn, the Leveller
from his Physick for Families, 1681

Reproduced by courtesy of the Curators of the Bodleian Library

THE
CONCERN FOR SOCIAL JUSTICE
IN THE PURITAN REVOLUTION

By
W. SCHENK, Ph.D.

ILLUSTRATED

LONGMANS, GREEN AND CO.
LONDON • NEW YORK • TORONTO

LONGMANS, GREEN AND CO. LTD.
6 & 7 CLIFFORD STREET, LONDON, W.1

NICOL ROAD, BOMBAY 1
17 CHITTARANJAN AVENUE, CALCUTTA 13
36A MOUNT ROAD, MADRAS 2

LONGMANS, GREEN AND CO., INC
55 FIFTH AVENUE, NEW YORK 3

LONGMANS, GREEN AND CO.
215 VICTORIA STREET, TORONTO 1

First published 1948

CODE NUMBER: 12195

PRINTED IN GREAT BRITAIN
BY WESTERN PRINTING SERVICES LTD., BRISTOL

IN MEMORIAM PATRIS

PREFACE

AMONG the debts which it is my duty and pleasure to acknowledge I must first mention the one I owe to the people who are described in this book. In the course of intensive research into their lives and works I have, as it were, made friends with them, and they have amply rewarded my labours. These men ("some of peculiar genius, all touched by a common genius") have taught me to see both past and present in a new light; getting to know them has enriched my life.

The dedication of this book seeks to express my gratitude to my father, whose love and kindness were unceasing and unbounded.

Next, I want to thank my mother for her loving care, her teaching, and her example; my wife for sharing my interests to the full and for much patient help; my brother for providing me with the vivid experience of brotherliness; and my sister-in-law for many stimulating suggestions. I also wish to record my gratitude for the generosity of Mr. and Mrs. Barclay Baron, who, after I had to leave Prague, enabled me to complete my studies in England.

Of my earlier teachers, I owe most to the late Dr. Eugen Lieben, who awakened my interest in history and social ethics, and taught me the meaning of justice and charity by living what he taught. My readers will have no difficulty in ascertaining that I have been powerfully influenced by the published writings of Ernst Troeltsch and R. H. Tawney. Professor Tawney has, in addition, helped me throughout by kind encouragement and invaluable advice. Like countless others, I owe much to Professor G. D. H. Cole: to his teaching as well as to his inspiring interest in the history of the common people. My contact with Dr. E. F. Jacob, under whose guidance I worked at Manchester University for two years, has been of great value to me; I have learnt much from his rich experience and urbane wisdom, even from his *obiter dicta*. Mr. Max Beloff, my other supervisor at Manchester, has read the complete manuscript and has helped me to avoid many errors both in subject-matter and presentation. My friend Professor L. C. Knights has, in the course of many enjoyable conversations and by his writings, greatly increased my insight into the civilisation of seventeenth-century England. During the last stage of my work I had the good fortune to meet Professor Wilhelm Flitner, of Hamburg University, who has strengthened my own conclusions and helped me to realise their wider significance.

My thanks are also due to the British Museum (and particularly to Dr. V. Scholderer) for not sparing any trouble in making the Thomason Collection accessible to me while it was stored away for safety; to the Bodleian Library for the use of its resources; to the John Rylands Library for much assistance and courtesy; and to Friends' House (London), Woodbrooke College (Birmingham), and Friends' Meeting House (Manchester) for the use, under very difficult conditions, of their extensive libraries of Quaker tracts.

I have not thought it necessary to compile yet another bibliography. The sources actually used are referred to in the notes; the general reader will not want any further information, and the specialist will know where to look for it. Most of the material on which this study is based can be found in the British Museum. I have tried to reproduce, as far as possible, the original spelling of the quotations, but I have modernised the punctuation wherever the meaning might otherwise have been in doubt.

It remains to thank the editors of the *Economic History Review*, the *Church Quarterly Review*, and *Humanitas*, for allowing me to make use of material published in these periodicals.

W.S.

University College of the South-West
 Exeter
October 1947

CONTENTS

ix

ILLUSTRATIONS

CHAPTER ONE

THE PROBLEM AND THE SETTING

OUR age, seething with revolutionary unrest, tends to discover its affinity with all revolutionary periods of the past. It is therefore not surprising that interest in the Puritan Revolution has been growing in recent years. Valuable research work on many aspects of the subject has resulted in a closer understanding of that eventful period between 1640 and 1660. We still think of it as an important stage in the history of English freedom, both political and religious, but we are also able to discern the outlines of a major social upheaval, breaking down old-established institutions and venerable traditions and so fostering the growth of modern society. Further, we are beginning to appreciate how deeply men's minds were affected by the complexity of their age. At no other time has there been in England such a prodigious crop of theoretical thinking on almost every conceivable question. Not only was the religious debate carried on with unheard-of intensity, but many problems of political theory that are familiar to us from present-day discussion make their unmistakable appearance during those years. In view of the patent disorders in state and government, the theoretical questions concerning political sovereignty and the "fundamental laws" of the country were not merely of academic interest. There were some men, moreover, who were thinking, not so much of a lawful government, but rather of a just society; who felt, in the Quaker sense of the word, a "concern" for social justice.

It is obvious why this interesting minority should find willing listeners in our own time. We should be in danger of misunderstanding our age if we failed to detect, behind much superficial verbiage, something which must on no account be lightly dismissed: the desire for social justice. Many of us feel that our society is very far removed from any idea we may have of a true community, and much of our activity is directed towards social reform and reconstruction. The social reformers of the seventeenth century can therefore easily be regarded as fore-runners of similar movements in modern times, and this view has in fact been put forward by a number of contemporary historians.[1]

Whenever we come across expressions of social unrest we are inclined to look for their cause among the prevailing material conditions of life. Though more work on this subject remains to be done, we have been helped by a succession of penetrating studies[2] to know the main outlines of the economic and social history of our period. There is, for example, a good deal of evidence that the years immediately preceding the revolution and some of the revolutionary years themselves witnessed an acute economic depression,[3] and it is known that certain social changes which had begun much earlier and were apt to cause economic distress were accelerated at that time. But it is very important to realise that a knowledge of trade cycles, wages and prices does not, in itself, enable us to explain social unrest. Whether people are content with their economic and social lot depends to some extent on their idea, however vaguely defined, of social justice. This idea, though not unin-fluenced by material factors, is not their inevitable reflection; the same material challenge need not always produce the same response. The social historian of the eighteenth century, for example, "is forced to catalogue a series of convincing reasons for discontent, and then to record contentment."[4] Similarly, historians have not reached agreement on just how hungry were the "Hungry Forties" of the nineteenth century, but the widespread social unrest during that period is an undeniable fact. Now we know that the idea of social justice prevalent in our own time is based on some such convictions as the natural equality of men and the paramount importance of the satisfac-tion of material desires in the pursuit of happiness; these beliefs, it need hardly be stressed, are also integral parts of the modern view of life. It is the chief aim of the present study to trace the corresponding beliefs and assumptions underlying the idea of social justice as it was voiced during the Puritan Revolution, and to show their connection with the currents of seventeenth-century thought. In other words we shall attempt to discover the nature of the radicals' inward response to the manifold challenges of the Puritan Revolution. History, according to R. G. Collingwood, means "getting into other people's heads," and this is what we intend to do.

Most of the men who will be heard in the following pages belonged to the middle or lower classes, and in quieter times such men do not leave much behind that allows us to know their minds. Often it is even impossible to discover what they were doing, let alone what they were thinking. Historians of the Puritan Revolution are more fortunate in possessing a collection of over 20,000 pamphlets assembled by the London bookseller, George Thomason, which includes the writings of those who do not normally commit their thoughts to paper. The picture which can be pieced together from these and other sources is quite remarkable. Although there is much familiar tavern-talk and some ado about nothing, there is also a great deal of worldly wisdom and spiritual illumination, and much of it is written in a lively and vigorous style, direct in narrative, supple in combat, and in sublimer moments inspired by the poetry of the Authorised Version. These men certainly deserve to be heard. Let us, by all means, praise famous men, but let us not neglect the obscure men: among them were our fathers who begat us. For a brief hour some of them will be the protagonists on our stage. But before we can listen to them, we must, like a good Prologue, describe the setting in which they are to move. It will, therefore, be necessary to remind ourselves of a few relevant facts about the age of Elizabeth and the early Stuarts.

The power of the Tudor monarchy rested on a firm foundation of popular approval. Elizabeth was quite entitled to address Parliament at the end of her life in those sonorous words which read like Shakespearean blank verse: "Though God hath raised me high, yet this I account the glory of my Crown, that I have reigned with your loves." Parliament, it is true, had in the last years of her reign shown some signs of restiveness, but on the whole, Parliament and people were quite willing to support a régime which was in its conception strongly paternal and could at times be ruthlessly despotic. There was little freedom in the sense in which this word came to be understood in later days. Economic activities were regulated by a complicated machinery of state and guild control; religious uniformity was imposed; freedom of speech in Parliament and immunity of members of Parliament from arrest were not guaranteed; the Privy Council exercised a fairly strict supervision over local administration; and new, or revived, Prerogative Courts (among them the Court of Star Chamber representing part of the jurisdiction of the Privy Council, and the Court of High Commission for ecclesiastical cases) served to enforce the monarch's will.

When early in the new century the Stuarts followed the Tudors, things began to change. James I was vain and tactless, and having reigned in Scotland since infancy, he knew little about the conditions in England. It appeared, moreover, that those who had willingly followed the leadership of the Tudors were now intending to assert themselves rather more strongly. A growing party in the House of Commons claimed a share in the government of the country, and they were supported by the Common Lawyers, led by Sir Edward Coke, who wanted to establish the superiority of the Common Law over the Prerogative Courts. The men who represented the shires and boroughs of England in the House of Commons were mostly members of a prosperous class of lesser landowners; many of them were also, directly or indirectly, interested in the growing commercial and industrial undertakings of the country. During the sixteenth century they had acquired much land. The Tudors, faced with a rapid rise of prices and the consequent extraordinary increase in the expenses of a government with constantly enlarging functions, had sold many of the lands which the Crown had acquired by the seizure of monastic and other property. Other big landowners, too, found it difficult to adapt their traditional methods to the price-revolution and had to sell

out. The new landlords (among whom were large-scale specu-
lators) were determined to exploit their lands to the full;
"improvement" was the watchword, and that meant regarding
the land solely as a source of profit, irrespective of the social
consequences. They were helped by the fact that in many cases
the legal rights of the tenants were uncertain. This applied
especially to those copyholders who held according to "the cus-
tom of the manor," a mode of possession not recognised by the
Common Law. So the new landlords were often able to raise
their tenants' rents or to replace them by others who would pay
according to the current market level. "The gentlemen," noted
a shrewd observer in 1600, "which were wont to addict themselves to the warres, are now for the most part growen to
become good husbandes and knowe [as] well how to improve
their lands to the uttermost as the farmer or countryman, so
that they take their farmes into their handes as the leases expire,
and eyther till themselves or else lett them out to those who
will give most."[5] Often they found it profitable to enclose their
lands and turn them over to pasture, and this type of enclosure,
by depriving many country people of their former employment,
caused much local economic distress. "Sheep," wrote Sir
Thomas More in a famous passage, "have become so great
devourers and so wild, that they eat up and swallow down the
very men themselves."[6] Other economic developments were
hardly less important. "The age of Elizabeth," to quote R. H.
Tawney's concise summary, "saw a steady growth of capitalism in textiles and mining, a great increase of foreign trade and
an outburst of joint-stock enterprise in connection with it, the
beginnings of something like deposit banking in the hands of
the scriveners, and the growth, aided by the fall of Antwerp
and the Government's own financial necessities, of a money
market with an almost modern technique—speculation, futures,
and arbitrage transactions—in London."[7]

With all this well-established and growing wealth came the
spirit of self-reliance and the desire for independence. In asserting themselves against the King, the members of the House of
Commons had very powerful financial weapons in their hands.

According to ancient usage, Parliament had to consent to any taxation required by the King in addition to his ordinary revenue, and, for the reasons set out above, the King became increasingly dependent on such additional sums. Parliament was more and more inclined to ask for the redress of grievances before it was prepared to supply the necessary taxes; to control the use of voted supplies; and to criticise, and sometimes to impeach, unpopular advisers of the King. All this came to a head early in Charles I's reign. Parliament refused Charles I the usual vote of the customs duties known as tonnage and poundage, and forced him, by threatening to withhold supplies, to agree to the Petition of Right (1628) which was intended to prevent unparliamentary taxation and arbitrary imprisonment. In the following year Charles dissolved his unruly Parliament and decided to rule without it. The King's main difficulty during this period of personal rule (1629–40) was, of course, financial. Depriving himself of normal taxation granted by Parliament he had to find other means of carrying on the government of the country. He used various more or less ingenious methods, most of which were old expedients of royal policy in times of need, such as forced loans, grants of monopoly patents, and collection of certain taxes despite the absence of parliamentary approval. The levy of one of these taxes, ship-money, has impressed itself for ever on the mind of posterity because of John Hampden's spirited stand against it. The granting of commercial and industrial monopolies, a less spectacular affair, was equally important. It affected a very large group of men: consumers complained of high prices and low quality, potential newcomers to the restricted trades found their way barred, and trespassers came into unpleasant contact with the Court of Star Chamber.

Charles' government has been as strongly praised by Clarendon as it has been condemned by the adherents of the "Whig interpretation of history." Whatever the final verdict, it is clear that Charles' policy was more than a series of makeshift arrangements for an arbitrary rule. It was fundamentally nothing else but the continuation of the paternal government of the Tudors. True, even beneficial measures had often a less respectable financial aspect, but the existence of a well-intentioned general policy is beyond doubt. Charles' Privy Council, just like that of the Tudors, tried to control the foreign exchange business, to regulate wages and prices, to check the enclosure movement, to protect the guilds of smaller craftsmen against exploitation by merchants, or to enforce the laws concerning poor relief. This policy was most conspicuously represented by William Laud, Archbishop of Canterbury since 1633 and, together with Strafford, Charles' most powerful adviser. Laud steadfastly opposed the contemporary tendency of separating private economic gain from considerations of public welfare, and in doing so he was clearly upholding the ancient teaching of the Church on these matters. But he also insisted, and that with great zeal, on the carrying out of another traditional principle, religious uniformity. He used the Prerogative Courts equally for the punishment of civil offences and the suppression of religious heterodoxy. Censorship of the press was strictly enforced, and offenders against it, like the Puritans Prynne and Lilburne, were liable to lose their ears or to be whipped at the cart's tail and to be imprisoned for an indefinite time.

When Prynne lost his first ear in 1634, for publishing a book against the theatres which was held to imply an attack on the theatre-loving Court, the people of London did not take much notice of his public punishment. But three and four years later, when Prynne and Lilburne were pilloried, they were fêted like heroes. The Laudian persecution, like many others of its kind, had the effect of strengthening the very forces it had meant to extinguish. The Puritans, that is, those who inclined towards a more radical Protestantism than was possible under the Elizabethan church settlement, did not, for a long time, intend to secede from the Church of England but would have been satisfied with internal modifications. During Laud's administration, however, some Puritans preferred to emigrate to America and others were driven into violent opposition to Church and State alike. Some other men who had no strong religious convictions followed the Puritans' example, because they shared the deep-rooted English dislike of clerical rule. There was, in addition, the equally deep-rooted fear of Popery, which had been aroused, in the earlier reign, by James' repeated attempts to conclude a Spanish alliance and was revived by Laud's ritualism and Charles' marriage to Henrietta Maria of France, a Catholic princess. Finally, Charles' financial policy, as even his apologists have to admit, was extremely inefficient. It has been estimated, for example, that out of 6s. increased cost paid by the consumer of monopoly goods only 10d. found its way into the Exchequer (the corresponding figure from Customs is 5s. out of 6s.).[8] As a consequence, Charles' means, hardly large enough to meet his normal requirements, were entirely insufficient in times of crisis. Such a crisis came in 1640.

In the spring of that year Charles found himself compelled to summon Parliament for the first time after eleven years, and to ask for funds, because Laud's attempt to make Presbyterian Scotland adopt the Anglican Prayer Book had resulted in a war with the Scots. Parliament, however, as was to be expected, refused to grant the King any money before the redress of their grievances. Charles made some concessions, but refused to yield on all points and dissolved this so-called "Short Parliament" after little more than three weeks. He concluded a temporary truce with the Scottish rebels and then tried to raise an army with his scanty means. The Scots routed his army and forced him to pay a large indemnity. Now he had to summon a new Parliament—known to us as the "Long Parliament," the most important assembly of the Puritan Revolution—which met in November 1640.

At first the temper of this House was not revolutionary, but its members were strongly determined to have their demands fulfilled. Its initial legislation has left a permanent mark on English affairs. Parliament was to be called at least every three years and not to be dissolved against its will; taxation without the consent of Parliament was outlawed; the Prerogative Courts were abolished, and this ensured, among many other results, the collapse of most, though not all, monopolies. In addition, the victims of the old régime were quickly released and their place was taken by Strafford and Laud who were impeached and imprisoned. Behind all this was the widespread conviction that the rule of the King had recently been arbitrary and that he had violated the "fundamental laws" of the Kingdom.

To many people it seemed that these events, so suddenly putting an end to the King's absolute power, were inaugurating a new age of justice and liberty. The exact meaning of these powerful words, never easy to determine, is especially elusive at a time when a new historical epoch is felt to begin, when it is "bliss . . . in that dawn to be alive." It was, to use Jakob Burckhardt's words, "the wedding-day of the revolution." Anything seemed possible, and in some circles hopes were running very high—the old will-o'-the-wisp of the millennium was again making its appearance. The end of the Laudian policy of repression brought all underground religious forces to the surface and engendered new ones in considerable strength. Without understanding them we should miss the full meaning of what is to follow in these pages.

Precisely what part was played by religion in the beginning of the Puritan Revolution is still an open question. J. W. Allen has pointed out that there is not much evidence of religious interest among the members of the Long Parliament or the majority of the writers pleading the Parliamentarian cause during the early 1640's.[9] Most of these men were country gentlemen, rich merchants, or prominent lawyers, and it is likely that these social groups had, more than others, absorbed the manifold secularising tendencies which had been gathering strength since the later Middle Ages. John Selden, himself an important member of the Long Parliament and a particularly clear-headed observer, took this for granted when he said: "Gentlemen have ever been more temperate in their religion than the common people, as having more reason, the others running in a hurry."[10] Many of these "gentlemen," to be sure, took their religion seriously enough, but they were accustomed to discuss political matters in secular terms. "Religion," Cromwell admitted in retrospect, "was not the thing at first contested for," but he went on: "God brought it to that issue at last, and gave it unto us by way of redundancy."[11] This happened, we may suggest, when the Parliamentarian revolt became a revolution by spreading, in the course of the Civil War, from the higher classes to their social inferiors.

The common people, our evidence leads us to believe,[12] were passionately interested in religious matters, and this at a time when a thorough knowledge of the Bible could be taken for granted. Many of them had probably never read any other book, or, being unable to read themselves, had only heard it read out by others, but this was sufficient to release an intense religious inquiry. The great Protestant touchstone was used to test the Church of England and the outcome could not be uncertain. The central issue of this conflict, as of similar ones in the past, has been admirably set out by Max Weber and Ernst Troeltsch, who have drawn attention to the fundamental differences between two types of religious bodies: the church and the sect.[13] A church is an all-embracing institution, claiming to embrace all the world in the case of the Roman Church, or all the nation in the case of her Protestant successor-churches. A sect, on the other hand, is a group of believers whose mature religious experiences have caused them to separate from those who do not share their degree of illumination. This was well expressed by one of the Puritan sectarians, John Lilburne, of whom we shall presently hear more. "The Church of England," he wrote in one of his inflammatory pamphlets, ". . . doeth not consist of true Believers . . . but of all sorts and kinds of wicked persons." The demands of the Gospel, in Lilburne's view, could only be fulfilled by a sect—"a company of believers who are washed in the blood of Christ by a free and voluntary consent in willingnesse to enter into that heavenly and holy State, City or Kingdom, which in the word of God is plentifully described."[14] It is obvious, therefore, why the question of infant baptism was of such paramount importance to the sectarians: membership of a church can be acquired by being the child of certain parents who act on the child's behalf, but membership of a sect depends on a voluntary act of a kind which can only be performed by an adult.

A consistent application of the sectarian idea raised many

problems. Perhaps the most important of these concerned the
question of Church government. The Scottish Puritans (the
Presbyterians) had vested a divinely delegated power in a
council of ministers and elders; they believed, as a contemporary
writer put it, that God's rule for His Church was "Aristocrati-
call by Elders, not Monarchicall by Bishops, nor Democrati-
call by the people."[15] They had also attempted to build up a
hierarchical organisation of assemblies ruling the Church as a
whole. The sectarians had very different views on these matters. They found their basis in Jesus' words: "Where two or
three are gathered together in my name, there am I in the
midst of them" (Matt. xviii, 20). Ecclesiastical power was held
to lie exclusively with the individual congregation. Such a body
of believers could, and did, enter into loose confederations with
similar groups, but there was no room for any hierarchy of
dignitaries or assemblies. One of the far-reaching consequences
of this development was the changed relation between the representatives of religion and the State; separation of Church and
State was necessarily insisted on by all sects. The idea of an
all-embracing national church was never to recover from this
crisis despite all the efforts of Presbyterian divines and Erastian
politicians. But if there was to be no national church there could
be no enforced maintenance of a national clergy by compulsory
tithes. The question of tithes was indeed constantly discussed
during the revolution. A believer in the sect-ideal must clearly
find it monstrous to have to contribute to the salaries of men
whose very office he cannot recognise and whose influence he is
apt to regard as pernicious. There were others, of course, who
simply wanted to get rid of tithes, without caring greatly for
either church or sect.

Other religious problems occupying the minds of the sectarians centred round Bunyan's haunting question: "How can I
be saved?" A Christian cannot but be concerned with his salvation, nor is this concern necessarily selfish, for he may know
that only true unselfishness will save him. But man is fallen
and so evidently the slave of sin: how then, in view of God's
justice, can he hope to escape damnation? What could all the

works of virtue avail if they were held against the evil so deeply ingrained in ourselves? And yet it was written that some would see eternal light. Only sheer grace could bring about the spiritual rescue of any man, and God's infinite majesty was so much beyond man's comprehension that one could not hope to discover why some men were singled out to be His companions. The awful and mysterious doctrine of Predestination was engaging the minds and emotions of the Puritans with remarkable force. But the strain imposed by this doctrine is so great that a reaction was inevitable. Some of the sectarians were and remained Calvinists, but another trend of thought was increasingly gaining ground among them. According to this view, too, salvation was not merited by fallen man; he could not justify himself in the sight of God. But Christ, by taking upon Himself the sins of the world, had achieved this justification, and thus salvation was offered to all who believed in Christ and not only to a few Elect. This doctrine of the justification by Christ gave renewed vigour to the latent tension between the two books of the Christian scriptures, because no event before Christ's coming was essential in this scheme of reconciliation between God and man. A tendency towards what is called, in theological language, Antinomianism was very noticeable: in various ways it was again asserted that the teachings of the Old Testament ("the Law," "*nomos*"), however valuable in their own time, had been entirely superseded by the Christian Gospel. This belief, too, was liable to lead men away from Calvinism. It has often been observed that orthodox Calvinism showed a marked affinity with the atmosphere of the Old Testament. Although the influence of the Old Testament was by no means absent among the sectarians (the example of the first Puritan generations was still powerful and much depended on the selection from that Book), it was certainly less outstanding. Calvinist righteousness was, to some extent, modified by the emphasis on the Gospel message of love.

All these spiritual forces were set free by the successful struggle of Parliament against the King. It is not our task to describe the gradual unfolding of this portentous conflict. In

August 1642 the King raised his standard in Nottingham and the Civil War began. At first the King's army had the better of the fighting. It was not until Oliver Cromwell raised and drilled his Puritan neighbours of the Eastern counties, "men as had the fear of God before them," that the Parliamentarian army began to be victorious. These "Ironsides" formed the nucleus of the New Model Army, which was established in 1645 and in the same year won the decisive victory at Naseby. Though it may well be true, as Richard Baxter reports, that "the greatest part of the common soldiers, especially of the foot, were ignorant men of little religion"[16] (the New Model consisted partly of pressed men), yet there also were in this army many vigorous sectarians whose zeal was strengthened by a group of enthusiastic and highly unorthodox chaplains.

In the course of 1646 this First Civil War came to an end, but further conflicts were developing among the victors. In that year a group of radical critics led by Lieutenant-Colonel John Lilburne, lately returned from the army, began to attack the policy of Parliament. They felt that, contrary to their earlier expectations, Parliament had not removed some of their major grievances. The Laudian persecution had indeed come to an end, but, like Milton, they found ample reason for believing that, with regard to religious intolerance, "New Presbyter is but Old Priest writ large." Because of the alliance with the Scots, indispensable during the war, an Assembly of Divines had been called to Westminster in order to consider the introduction of the Presbyterian system into England. These clergymen were horrified by the outbreak of sectarianism and unauthorised preaching, and Parliament was quite prepared to help them by passing laws against heresy, by burning heretical books, and by forbidding laymen to preach—all this, as one of these critics remarked, "by the instigation of a clergy no more infallible than the former."[17] Other complaints concerned a particularly obnoxious monopoly, that of the powerful Merchant Adventurers, which had been confirmed in 1643; the growing burden of taxation; and the lack of personal security as shown by the imprisonment of Lilburne by the House of Lords. Early in 1647 these men produced a petition containing a list of their grievances, collected signatures, and presented it to the House of Commons, which promptly ordered it to be burned by the hangman.

A similar spirit of disaffection towards Parliament arose in the victorious army. The House of Commons intended to disband the army and to ask the disbanded soldiers to re-enlist for service in Ireland, without, however, making adequate provisions for the considerable arrears of pay due to the army or giving any other guarantees. The answer of the common soldiers was unprecedented: in April and May 1647 the soldiers of each regiment elected their own representatives, called Agitators, to look after their interests. The army leaders concurred by establishing an Army Council, consisting, in addition to the general officers, of two soldiers and two officers from each regiment. In June 1647 the King, at that time in the hands of Parliament, was seized by Cornet Joyce's famous coup, and in August, making use of dissensions within Parliament, the army entered London and forced its stoutest opponents among the members of Parliament to leave the country. Soon, however, it became evident that the army itself was not united. At some time during the spring or summer of 1647 the Agitators had joined hands with the radical civilian group round Lilburne, whose writings are known to have had a great influence in the army. The two groups together produced a set of proposals called the " Agreement of the People," and this document was discussed in the Army Council at Putney in October and November 1647. These debates, now justly famous, centred round the radicals' demand for universal franchise as the natural birthright of every Englishman. The spokesman for the opposing view was Henry Ireton, Cromwell's son-in-law, a very able debater with a cold and piercing intelligence. He suggested that only those who had "a permanent fixed interest in this kingdom" should have the vote, "that is, the persons in whom all land lies, and those in corporations in whom all trading lies."[18] The army leaders, in spite of their quarrel with Parliament, had evidently no intention of undermining its social basis: the landed gentry and the big merchants.

It was the alliance of the civilian radicals with the Agitators that produced the party of the Levellers (so named, according to Lilburne, by Cromwell and Ireton at Putney).[19] In the eventful years 1647–9 the Leveller movement was the rallying-point of almost all those who had set high hopes on the revolution and were now bitterly disappointed. To discover the nature of this discontent will be the aim of the three succeeding chapters; its outward history can be briefly told here. The Putney debates ended in disagreement, and officers and Agitators alike were dismissed to their respective regiments. On 15th November there was an outbreak of mutiny in two regiments at a rendezvous near Ware, but Cromwell restored discipline by dashing amongst the soldiers with his sword drawn; one of the mutineers was shot. In the following months the Levellers were especially active in London, building up a distinct party organisation with agents throughout the kingdom, voluntary contributions from the members, frequent meetings, and still more frequent pamphlets. From July 1648 to September 1649 they even published their own news-sheet (the *Moderate*) which, in addition to printing all the news of interest to Levellers, contained leading articles on Leveller ideas. It was intended that the first public activity of the party should be the presenting of a new petition to Parliament, but in January 1648 the chief promoters of this petition, the indefatigable John Lilburne and his associate John Wildman, were arrested after one of the preparatory meetings in Smithfield.

From May to August 1648 the army was involved in fresh fighting: this time against the Scots who had come to terms with the King and now attempted to restore him to power, and against dangerous local insurrections in Kent and Wales. As soon as this Second Civil War was over, Leveller activities flared up again. A comprehensive petition was presented to Parliament on 11th September 1648, and a new version of the "Agreement of the People" was drawn up in consultation with the other political groups. This agreement was again discussed with the army leaders who wanted to make sure of a wide support for their bold plans, which they realised in rapid succession from December 1648 onwards: the purge of Parliament, leaving only a small minority of army adherents (nicknamed the Rump); the trial and execution of the King (the symbolic act that made Europe shudder); and the establishment of a republic. The Levellers, as was to be expected, were violently opposed to these steps which made the rule of the army leaders absolute; the political reality of 1649 was obviously a mockery of the professed principle that "the people under God are the original of all power." Lilburne published a number of pamphlets full of the most bitter invective, and in March 1649 he and three of his associates were arrested by a heavy guard of soldiers and brought before the Council of State. On this occasion, Cromwell, so we are told by Lilburne who claims to have overheard the General through a door, told the Council of State, "thumping his fist upon the Council Table, til it rang": "You have no other way to deale with these men, but to break them in pieces, . . . if you do not break them, they will break you."[20] The Leveller leaders were imprisoned in the Tower, and a series of mutinies in the army in April and May 1649 was finally crushed by Cromwell at Burford and followed by the execution of three ringleaders. In the struggle for power the Levellers, like the King, were defeated by force:

> The same arts that did gain
> A power must it maintain.

Here the Leveller movement came to an end. Individual Levellers were still active behind the scenes, but no more concerted actions or new ideas were to come from this group. Cromwell was, in any case, too firmly established in power for any large-scale opposition movement to be possible. He dismissed even the remnant of the Long Parliament in 1653 and then tried various constitutional experiments, but he was never able to conceal the fact that his power rested on a military foundation. The vexatious régime of the Major-Generals in particular has impressed itself forcefully on the memory of Englishmen. Cromwell died in 1658 and his work did not survive him for long. In the course of 1659–60 a tumultuous and somewhat ludicrous drama was played out, almost exactly reversing the earlier sequence of events: restoration of the Rump (with a confused interlude of renewed military rule), restoration of the Long Parliament, and finally restoration of the Stuart Monarchy. On 29th May 1660 Charles II, the son of the royal martyr, entered London, greeted by an enthusiastic crowd.

To all these kaleidoscopic changes in the course of twenty years must be added much economic and social dislocation. The lands of Church and Crown and of some Royalists were confiscated and many Royalists were forced to sell some or all of their lands in one way or another. Some people were getting very rich by land speculation or by lending money to the State in exchange for confiscated lands. Others managed to increase their wealth by using their membership of local tax-committees to divert some of the taxes into their own pockets; the name committeeman had a notorious ring during those years. If some were rapidly rising in the social scale, many others must have found it difficult or impossible not to fall. Owing to the cost of maintaining army and navy, taxation was far higher than at any previous time, and a new indirect tax, excise, bore especially hard on the poorer classes; prices were very high, particularly in 1648 and 1649; both foreign and domestic trade were seriously disturbed by the Civil War; there was an outbreak of enclosure riots in the early 1640's; and there is plenty of evidence that the relief of the poor was a pressing social problem throughout these years.[21] These evils were aggravated by the fact that the Interregnum governments did practically nothing to replace the Stuart machinery dealing with such matters as enclosures and poor relief; the ear of Parliament was "impenetrably closed to agrarian grievances," and the general impression left by the Poor Law policy "is that of harshness coupled with failure."[22] Underlying these policies was a far-reaching change of influential opinion concerning these social problems. The prevailing view was now that any interference with enclosures was a curtailment of property rights and that poverty was largely due to idleness and lack of thrift. There were a few exceptions (notably Richard Baxter, who firmly

C

upheld the traditional social teaching of the Church), but the social thought of most leading men on the Puritan side was of this kind.

So much then for the setting of our study. Let us now listen to the Puritan radicals, to the village Hampdens and inglorious Miltons, for once not mute.

NOTES TO CHAPTER ONE

[1] E. Bernstein, *Sozialismus und Demokratie in der grossen Englischen Revolution* (1895)—English translation: *Cromwell and Communism* (1930); T. C. Pease, *The Leveller Movement* (1916); W. Haller, *Tracts on English Liberty* (1934), vol. i; H. J. Laski, *The Rise of European Liberalism* (1936); C. Hill (ed.), *The English Revolution, 1640* (1940), particularly the essays by C. Hill and M. James; D. W. Petegorsky, *Left-Wing Democracy in the English Civil War* (1940). Much of the primary material of this subject is now accessible in excellent modern editions: W. Haller, *Tracts on English Liberty* (1934), vols. ii, iii; A. S. P. Woodhouse, *Puritanism and Liberty* (1938); G. H. Sabine, *The Works of Gerrard Winstanley* (1941); and W. Haller and G. Davies, *Leveller Tracts, 1647–1653* (1944). W. Haller, A. S. P. Woodhouse and G. H. Sabine have all added most valuable introductions to their respective editions (cf. also W. Haller, *The Rise of Puritanism*, 1938). I am particularly indebted to A. S. P. Woodhouse's comprehensive and stimulating essay. The standard works of S. R. Gardiner and C. H. Firth are still, and are likely to remain, the indispensable basis of all work in this field.

[2] The following are particularly important: G. Unwin, *Industrial Organization in the Sixteenth and Seventeenth Centuries* (1904); W. Scott, *Joint Stock Companies* (1910–12); R. H. Tawney, *The Agrarian Problem in the Sixteenth Century* (1912); E. Lipson, *A History of the Woollen and Worsted Industries* (1921); S. Liljegren, *The Fall of the Monasteries* (1924); M. James, *Social Problems and Policy during the Puritan Revolution* (1930); F. C. Dietz, *English Public Finance, 1558–1641* (1932); J. U. Nef, *The Rise of the British Coal Industry* (1932); E. Lipson, *The Economic History of England* (1934, etc.); J. U. Nef, "The Progress of Technology and the Growth of Large Scale Industry in Great Britain, 1540–1640," *Economic History Review*, Oct. 1934; C. Hill, "The Agrarian Legislation of the Interregnum," *Economic History Review*, April 1940; R. H. Tawney, "The Rise of the Gentry, 1558–1640," *Economic History Review*, vol. xi, No. 1, 1941.

[3] M. James, *Social Problems and Policy, passim.*

[4] G. D. H. Cole and R. Postgate, *The Common People* (1938), p. 95.

[5] Thomas Wilson, "The State of England A.D. 1600," ed. F. J. Fisher, *Camden Miscellany*, vol. xvi, 18.

[6] *Utopia* (Everyman's edition), p. 23.

[7] R. H. Tawney, *Religion and the Rise of Capitalism* (1926), p. 176. Cf. also J. U. Nef's article in the *Economic History Review*, Oct. 1934.

[8] W. Scott, op. cit., i, 22.

[9] J. W. Allen, *English Political Thought, 1604–1644* (1938), p. 457.

[10] Selden's *Table-Talk*, under "Gentlemen."

[11] Speech to the First Protectorate Parliament, 22nd Jan. 1655.

12 On the prodigious outburst of popular religion in the early 1640's, see especially the relevant chapters of W. Haller's *Rise of Puritanism*.

13 Max Weber, *Gesammelte Aufsätze zur Religionssoziologie*, vol. i (1920), partly translated into English in *The Protestant Ethic and the Spirit of Capitalism* (1930); Ernst Troeltsch, *Die Soziallehren der christlichen Kirchen und Gruppen* (1912)—English translation: *The Social Teaching of the Christian Churches* (1931).

14 John Lilburne, *Answer to Nine Arguments* (written 1638, published 1645), pp. 11, 28.

15 John Geree, *The Character of an old English Puritane, or Non-Conformist* (1646), p. 4.

16 *Reliquiae Baxterianae* (1696), p. 53.

17 William Walwyn, *Petition* (March 1647), printed in Woodhouse, op. cit. p. 319.

18 Woodhouse, op. cit., pp. 53, 54.

19 *L. Colonel John Lilburne His Apologeticall Narration* (1652), p. 70, and Woodhouse, op. cit. p. 351. It is possible that Charles I was the first to use this name; cf. his Declaration from Hampton Court, 11th Nov. 1647, where he refers to "the levellers' doctrine," and Mercurius Pragmaticus, 9–16th Nov. 1647: "We must leave off the names of Adjutators [i.e. Agitators] now, and take up a new one, since his Majesty in his Declaration hath christned these Pagan Counsellors by the name of Levellers."

20 Lilburne, *Picture of the Councel of State* (1649), pp. 14–15.

21 M. James, *Social Problems and Policy*, contains much interesting material on all these points. The statements in the text attempt to summarise some of M. James' conclusions.

22 R. H. Tawney, *Religion and the Rise of Capitalism*, p. 258; M. James, *Social Problems and Policy*, p. 272.

CHAPTER TWO

JOHN LILBURNE: THE AGREEMENT OF THE PEOPLE

TABLE OF LEVELLER DATES

1647	March–May	First (Large) Petition to Parliament
	April–May	Agitators elected
	October–November	Putney Debates (Army Council) on First Agreement of the People
	15th November	Mutiny at Ware
1648	January	Increasing Leveller propaganda Smithfield Petition prepared Lilburne and Wildman imprisoned
	11th September	Petition to Parliament
	November	Second Agreement of the People
	December	Whitehall Debates (Council of Officers)
1649	30th January	Execution of Charles I
	23rd March	Imprisonment of Leveller leaders
	April–May	Mutinies

JOHN LILBURNE, the most popular and most turbulent of the Leveller leaders, came from a Durham family who had owned lands in the North for centuries;[1] his maternal grandfather had been Yeoman of the Wardrobe to Queen Elizabeth. Being a younger son, he was apprenticed to a cloth merchant in London, with whom he stayed until about 1636. In London he came to be drawn into the religious activities of the pre-revolutionary years. In 1638, when he was twenty-four at the most,[2] he was charged with having taken part in printing a book against the Laudian church government and sentenced by the Star Chamber to be publicly whipped and to stand in the pillory. On this occasion, transforming the pillory into a platform, he

20

Mr Iohn Lilburn, a pious young Gentleman, of about 22 or 23 yeares of age for suspition of printing & divulging certain of Dr Bastwickes & other bookes. against Popish innovations. was censured in the Starr-Chamber to be whipt at a Carts-tayle from the ffleet to Westminster, had therby about 200 lashes with a whip, was then, presently upon it set on a pillorie, with a gagg in his mouth. was fined 500ᵗ and kept close-prisoner in the ffleet where day & night hee lay in iron-shacles, and long time indured most barbarous and cruel usage:

JOHN LILBURNE
from an Engraving by Hollar

made an impassioned speech to the excited London crowd. Having discovered that he was able to hold its attention, he continued to do so for about twenty years. From now on he turned everything that happened to him into a public event, either by some spectacular action or by writing one of his innumerable pamphlets, which were greatly feared by the authorities. This stream of tracts could evidently not be checked, although he spent altogether eight years of his life in prison; it was, in fact, "utterly impossible to deprive him of ink."[3]

It is true that Lilburne possessed the gift of self-dramatisation to a high degree, but his life was certainly not devoid of truly dramatic incidents. After his cruel punishment he was kept in prison until he was released by the intervention of the Long Parliament, together with other victims of the Laudian persecution. After the outbreak of the Civil War he joined the Parliamentarian Army, full of unbounded enthusiasm for the cause of "God's true religion" against the "divellish" Cavaliers.[4] It was to be expected that Lilburne's military career would be one of bravery, if not of circumspection. Quite early in the campaign he was captured by the Cavaliers and was put on trial by them for high treason. He would have been condemned to death had not Parliament intervened once more and secured his release by way of exchange. In 1644 he captured Tickhill Castle by a bold stroke of his own without waiting for orders from his commanding officer, the Earl of Manchester, who was inclined to take disciplinary action against him. He was altogether on bad terms with Manchester, suspecting him, not without reason, of being only a half-hearted adherent of Parliament. Because of these quarrels he left the Army in 1645, having risen to the rank of Lieutenant-Colonel, but his troubles with his former chief were not over. For spreading libels about Lord Manchester, Lilburne was kept in prison by the House of Lords from 1646 to 1647. This was by no means the only powerful group with which he came into conflict; before long, he began to charge Parliament and the Army leaders, including Cromwell, with having shamefully betrayed the "Legall Fundamentall Liberties" of the English nation (the "good old cause" of the early 1640's), ascribing to them the worst motives of greed and ambition. For one of his most violent attacks Cromwell had him imprisoned in the Tower from March to July 1649, during that very critical stage of the new régime immediately after the execution of Charles I. He was charged with treason, but a London jury acquitted him in October 1649 amid popular rejoicings. After an unsuccessful start in business he now followed an old inclination of his and, "being dayly applyed unto for Counsel by friends," he began "to undertake men's honest causes, and to manage them either as Sollicitor or Pleader."[5] This "upstart monstrous Lawyer," as he was called by William Prynne, even tried to enter one of the Inns of Court, but an old adversary of his, the lawyer Prideaux, refused to admit him.[6] Once again he excelled in the gentle art of making enemies by crossing swords, on behalf of his uncle, with the influential politician Sir Arthur Hesilrige, about the possession of some Durham collieries. Lilburne, true to his habit, brought the gravest personal accusations against his opponent who, whatever the merits of his case, was sufficiently powerful to have the restless trouble-maker exiled from England. After the dissolution of the Rump Parliament in 1653, Lilburne returned to England from Flanders although he had not been pardoned, and consequently was arrested at once. His case was decidedly bad, but his brilliant oratory again succeeded in persuading the jury to acquit him. This time, however, he was not released and had to remain in various prisons for three more years. It was not until 1656 that he was given his freedom when he had adopted the pacifist beliefs of Quakerism and the Government, after an initial hesitation, had accepted his conversion as sincere. Soon afterwards, in August 1657, he died, little more than forty years old.

Lilburne was clearly not an easy man to get on with. He was short-tempered, and his suspicions were all too easily roused (it is not surprising to hear that he was also easily moved to tears[7]). An anonymous biographical sketch, published in the year of his death, describes him not unjustly as having been "of a high and undaunted Spirit, of a quick and pregnant Apprehension, of an excellent memory, but al wayes extreamly addicted to contention, a lover of novelties, an opposer of Government, unsettled in his judgement, and violent and bitter in his expressions."[8] Clarendon went further and spoke slightingly of Lilburne's "appetite for martyrdom," but one of his friends likened him to "a candle lighted, accomodating others, and consuming himself."[9] In any case, we must ask ourselves: What was the fire that burnt this candle to the ground? What was it that drove this man to a restless life and an early death?

Even one of Lilburne's bitterest opponents had to admit that his followers "look upon him as a Martyr in the Cause against the Bishops, and believe that all his zeal is only for the promotion of Righteousnesse and just things, and for the Vindicating and Asserting [of] the people's liberty against Oppression and Violence."[10] For many years the news-sheets of the capital were full of his adventures; all accounts, both the hostile and the friendly ones, testify to his outstanding popularity. Before leaving England on being banished he had supper with two hundred of his friends, many of whom accompanied him on horseback for several miles.[11] During all his trials many petitions on his behalf were presented to Parliament, and in 1653 "tickets were circulated with the legend:

And what, shall then honest John Lilburne die?
Three score thousand will know the reason why.

The Government filled London with troops, but in spite of their officers, the soldiers shouted and sounded their trumpets when they heard Lilburne was acquitted."[12] The other members of the audience were no less enthusiastic: they "gave such a loud and unanimous shout, as is believed, was never heard in Yeeld-hall, which lasted about half an hour without intermission."[13] On the same occasion, we are told, many Londoners "of the middle sort" appointed a public day of thanksgiving.[14] To these people Lilburne must have been the incarnated spirit of the Puritan Revolution, with its characteristic ideas of righteousness and liberty. It was certainly in this light that Lilburne saw himself and wanted to be seen by others. "The most faithful servants of Christ," he wrote, ". . . being ever the greatest enemies to tyranny and oppression, and the most zealous maintainers of the known laws and liberties of their Country, as was John Hus in Bohemia, Jerom of Prague, John Wickliff in England, the Martyrs in Queen Maryes dayes, the Hugonots or Protestants in France, the Gues in the Low-Countreys, [were] all not only esteemed Hereticks by the Church, but rebels and traytors to their several States and Princes. . . . Though I have not wherewith to compare with those glorious witnesses of God, . . . yet I have the assurance of God in my own conscience, that in the day of the Lord I shall be found to have been faithful."[15] This interesting passage reveals the historical place which Lilburne assigned to himself: that of a Protestant fighter for the cause of God and the liberties of the people, in the famous line of succession popularised by Foxe's *Book of Martyrs*.

Lilburne's conversion and first true approach to God—the most important event in the life of a Puritan—took place in 1636 when he joined a congregation of Calvinistic Baptists.[16] His most intimate friend at that time was William Kiffin (later to become one of the most prominent Baptists) who has left us a vivid account of those early days of their intense search for truth. "I began to get acquainted with several young men," he writes, "who diligently attended on the means of grace. It pleased God to make known much of himself and his grace unto them. And, being apprentices as well as myself, they had no opportunity of converse, but on the Lord's days. It was our constant practice to attend the morning lecture, which began at six o'clock. . . . We also appointed to meet together an hour before service, to spend it in prayer, and in communicating to each other, what experience we had received from the Lord; or else to repeat some sermon which we had heard before. After a little time, we also read some portion of Scripture, and spake from it what it pleased God to enable us."[17] It is necessary to be aware of Lilburne's religious zeal in order to appreciate the importance of his extraordinary spiritual experiences during his public punishment in 1638. "My soule," he wrote shortly afterwards, "was that morning exceedingly lifted up with spiritual consolation. . . . The executioner . . . tyed my hands . . . which caused me to utter these words, Wellcome be the Crosse of Christ. . . . When the first stripe was given I felt not the least paine but said, Blessed be thy name, O Lord my God, that hast counted mee worthy to suffer for thy glorious name's sake, And at the giving of the second, I cried out with a loud voice, Hallelujah, Hallelujah, Glory, Honour, and Praise, bee given to thee, O Lord for ever. . . . And this I counted my wedding day in which I was married to the Lord Jesus Christ." When he addressed the multitude from the pillory he felt that he spoke "in the name of the Lord, being assisted with the spirit and power of the God of Heaven and earth."[18]

This experience made an indelible impression on his mind. Many years afterwards, in 1656, he still referred to his "glorying and rejoycing condition under the bishops" and God's "mercy and indeared loving kindness" in his "great straits in the Bishops time."[19] It may have been as a result of this that he gained the assurance—so necessary to a Puritan—of being among the elect by predestination. "I honour and glorifie my God," he wrote soon after his punishment, "who hath passed by so many thousands as he hath done, and left them in their sins, and yet hath chosen me freely before the foundation of the world was laid."[20] He always regarded himself as "one that owned, and sensibly enjoyed by faith, the choicest of spiritual Union and communion with the Lord of life and glory."[21] His enemies were therefore, in the true Puritan fashion, not only wrong but wicked as well; they were enemies of Christ, sons of Satan, "perverters of Truth, Justice, and all kinds of Righteousnesse."[22]

Lilburne's attitude at the beginning of the Civil War was common among the Puritan adherents of Parliament, most of whom would have agreed with the "Fundamental Laws and Rights of the Nation," or whatever other name they would have chosen for their political aims. "The true religion," was Lucy Hutchinson's opinion, "was fenced with the liberty of the people, and so linked together, that it was impossible to make them slaves, till they were brought to be idolaters of royalty and glorious lust; and as impossible to make them adore these gods, while they continued loyal to the government of Jesus Christ."[23] For posterity, this interdependence of Puritan religion and politics is most memorably represented by Oliver Cromwell, and it is quite legitimate to think of him when we are discussing Lilburne. Cromwell, evidently impressed by Lilburne's martyrdom, devoted his first speech in the Long Parliament to supporting Lilburne's petition for release from imprisonment. The two men probably got to know each other in the army, and when Cromwell charged the Earl of Manchester with slackness in the prosecution of the war, Lilburne was one of his witnesses. At that time, in 1644 and 1645, Cromwell was Lilburne's "most intimate and familiar bosome friend";[24] as late as 1647, shortly before they became estranged, Lilburne wrote to Cromwell: "I have apprehended in you . . . an affectionate, cordiall, and free hearted spirit to the poore people of God."[25] The special bitterness of their later political feud must have been partly due to the very fact that they had been friends. In addition, there was on both sides an element of personal rivalry in this struggle of the popular soldier with the hardly less popular pamphleteer. The latter was known to have a large number of followers among the private soldiers and reminded his opponents that his following was as considerable as that of anyone else in England, "not excepting your very General."[26] In a typical passage, Lilburne appealed to God to do justice between him and Cromwell, and he prayed: "Deliver me from . . . thy once seeming servant Cromwel, who is visibly become . . . an Apostate from thee, an Enemy to thee, and a desperate persecutor of thee."[27] This is the kind of language which would have come as easily to Cromwell and which he may well have used about Lilburne; he did, at any rate, say that most of the Levellers were "such as have apostatised from their holy profession, such as being corrupt in their consciences have been forsaken by God."[22] Lilburne's and Cromwell's family likeness, in friendship as well as in enmity, is apparent; to us they are "united in the strife which divided them." (T. S. Eliot, *Little*

Gidding.) Living in the age of the Puritan Rebellion, both of them were Puritan rebels *par excellence*.

In yet another respect Lilburne was a typical protagonist of the Parliamentary cause: like Hampden and Pym and countless others he tended to think of the conflict in legal terms. He was, as we have seen, something of a would-be lawyer himself. Pym's famous panegyric on law ("The Law is that which puts a difference between good and evill, betwixt just and unjust. If you take away the Law, all things will fall into confusion," etc.) made such an impression on him that he seems to have known it by heart.[29] A generation earlier Sir Edward Coke had preached this worship of law, and it was to Coke's *Institutes*, especially to its second part, that Lilburne owed much of his outlook. Out of that book he preached "law and justice" to a crowd outside the House of Commons in 1648; it was lying on his table when a visitor came to see him in the Tower;[30] and it appears in his hands in one of the two pictures we have of him. Long stretches of Lilburne's pamphlets consist of extracts from Coke's work. Whenever he was in prison, he was particularly fond of quoting Coke's well-known exposition of the 29th chapter of Magna Carta: "No man shall be dispossessed of his life, limb, liberty or estate, but by due processe of Law."

Although this reverence for law was supported by a strong secular tradition, it had, in Lilburne's case, a religious source as well. As a Calvinist, he was strongly aware of "Adam's sin . . . which brought the curse upon him and all his posterity."[31] The result of this curse was that all men, if left to themselves, would be "more brutish, bloudy, and barbarous, than the brutishest or savagest of wilde Beasts." It was, therefore, necessary to restrain them by laws which should be devised "with a sinister opinion of all Mankinde as supposing it impossible for a just man to be born," so that "as little as possible . . . should be left to the discretion, will or pleasure of the Administrator."[32] Only in this way could order be established in a world of fallen men.

Lilburne's indebtedness to Coke includes an important idea which came to be widely discussed in the later 1640's: the con-

viction that England, ever since 1066, had been under the
"Norman yoke."[33] He may have found a good deal of support
for this view in the popular histories of England which he knew
well and quoted at great length. They are all surprisingly anti-
Norman, especially in their treatment of William the Conqueror's legal institutions. William Martyn's *The Historie and
Lives of the Kings of England*, published in 1638, contains the
statement that William the Conqueror "tired out the English
Nation with extraordinarie troubles and excessive charges in
the prosecution of their suits in Law"[34] and similar complaints
occur in the works of Holinshed, Speed and Daniel. Coke himself had based his theory on an old law-book of the thirteenth
century, called the *Mirrour of Justices*, which professed "to set
forth the ancient laws and usages, derived from Holy Writ, by
which the Saxons had governed themselves before the coming of
the Norman."[35] This idealisation of the Saxon past was taken up
by Coke; according to him the Saxon laws lived on in the
Common Law and had been imposed on the Norman rulers in
Magna Carta. From all this, Lilburne drew a number of conclusions, some of which, however, would hardly have met with
Coke's approval.

The King's authority, Lilburne argued bluntly, was derived
from "William the Invader and Robber, and Tyrant, alias the
Conqueror," and therefore from "the pernitious springs of
Robbery, Pyracie, Violence, and Murder." This applied also
to the House of Lords, because the Norman kings had made
"Dukes, Earles, Barrons, and Lords of their fellow Robbers,
Rogues and Theeves."[36] The royal ambitions had been success-
fully checked by such "gallant" laws as Magna Carta, the
Petition of Right and the Act abolishing the Star Chamber.
This body of statute law was therefore the "just, established,
unrepealed, fundamentall law of the Land."[37] But much that
went by the name of law was merely an "oppressing bondage"
having "come in by the will of a Tyrant . . . and his sword."[38]
He seems to have had in mind mainly the procedure of the
Common Law Courts, and this was indeed the object of a most
widespread and persistent grievance. His list of complaints can

be found again and again in contemporary writings. He attacked the "tediousnesse, ambiguities, uncertainties" of the legal system; "the entryes in Latine (as bad as the French)"; the rule that only professional lawyers (nearly all of them corrupt and greedy, "the vermine, plagues and pests of a Common wealth") were allowed to plead in Court; and the irksome necessity "to come from all places of the Kingdome, to seek for justice at Westminster."[39] All these were Norman practices, and until they were removed England was under the "Iron Norman Yoak."[40]

Against these Norman abuses Lilburne set his picture of Anglo-Saxon legal procedure. He seems to have owed it mainly to a passage from Samuel Daniel's *History of England* where the following Anglo-Saxon law is quoted: "All matters in question should . . . be finally decided in Gemote or Conventions held monethly in every hundred." To restore this practice Lilburne suggested that a local court should be formed in every hundred, "for the ending of all differences arising in that hundred, annually chosen by freemen of that hundred."[41] Except for a general supervision exercised by Parliament, this radical change would have brought to an end all central jurisdiction and, of course, all interference by professional lawyers. It would have meant an extension of the jury system—that arcanum of English liberties regarded as a survival of Saxon times—to all cases of law.

Lilburne's legal armoury would not have been complete if it had not included the much discussed idea of natural law. Not given to philosophical speculations, he was not interested in it from a theoretical point of view; to him the law of nature, in accordance with the traditional teaching, was the "Law of God, ingraven in nature and demonstrated by reason."[42] But what were the principles of that law? Like most adherents of the *lex naturae*, Lilburne was none too explicit on this point; much of what he has to say is merely political rhetoric. But his fundamental line of thought is clear enough: political authority could only rest on mutual consent; the King's arbitrary government had broken "the compact betwixt him and his people," and the people were therefore entitled by the law of nature to resist him with armed force in order to preserve themselves.[43]

So far Lilburne was in substantial agreement with most of the writers arguing the case of Parliament against the King, such as John Pym or Henry Parker. Again and again he turned to Pym's speech on Strafford's impeachment (which, he thought, contained an exposition of "the end and foundation of government")[44] and to Parker's *Observations upon some of his Majesty's late Answers and expresses* (July 1642). He was quite entitled to say: "if . . . I be called a State Heritage, I answer for my selfe, that the Parliaments own Declarations hath made me so and that if I be deluded and deceived, they are the men that have done it."[45]   But when men like Henry Parker spoke of the sovereignty and rights of the people, they thought—although they may not have said so explicitly—of the people as represented by their traditional spokesmen, the members of the House of Commons. They did not envisage any conflict between Parliament and people, and they did not claim the right of rebellion for every individual. While they advocated what they believed to be liberty, they were far from believing in equality of any kind. It is precisely at this point that Lilburne parted with their company. He did proclaim equality in the following "General Proposition"[46] which gives us an interesting insight into his political thought: "God, the absolute Sovereign Lord and King, the originall fountain and cause of all causes, who is circumscribed, governed and limited by no rules, but doth all things meerly and only by his sovereign will and unlimited good pleasure, who made the world and all things therein for his own glory," created Adam and Eve, "the earthly, originall fountain . . . of all and every particular and individuall man and woman . . . in the world since, who are . . . by nature all equall and alike in power, dignity, authority and majesty, none of them having (by nature) any authority, dominion, or magisteriall power one over or above another." Once again, a connection in Lilburne's mind between religion and politics becomes apparent. It is worth noting that his idea of equality was closely connected with the Calvinist conception of God's infinite majesty and unlimited power; it was not derived from the brotherhood of all men proclaimed in the Gospels. A violation of this equality was condemned by Lilburne, not because of its unbrotherliness, but because it was an attempt to be like God, "which was the sinne of the Devils."[47]

Whatever the background of his belief in equality, it is clear that Lilburne had in mind a new and revolutionary meaning when he spoke of the "people of England." According to him, the people consisted of free and equal individuals who, when political society was dissolved (and this he believed to be the case in 1647), were called upon to reconstitute it by a new social contract. Such an "Agreement of the People" would guarantee everybody's inalienable birthright not to submit to any authority without previous consent. Lilburne's fully developed political ideas rested on the conception of the individual voluntarily limiting his originally unlimited freedom. A direct consequence of these ideas is, of course, universal manhood suffrage.[48]

Here we are entering the world of modern democracy. It is understandable that this unheard-of proposal met with fierce opposition. The poor—so ran the argument of the opponents—are in a majority; if they are to have the vote and if the will of the majority is to prevail, who is to prevent them from equalising the property of all men or abolishing private property altogether?[49] These were, in fact, the designs with which Lilburne's followers were charged; their nickname "Levellers" was meant to suggest this danger. We shall have to discuss in a later chapter how far such ideas may have circulated among the Levellers, but in Lilburne's writings there is not a shred of evidence for ascribing to him the desire to abolish private property or to "level men's estates." On the contrary, he was a strong and consistent advocate of the institution of private property. He explicitly disavowed "the erronious tenents of the poor Diggers at Georgehill in Surrey"[50] and he even advanced the doctrine which was to gain so much ground in the eighteenth and nineteenth centuries that common ownership "would destroy . . . all industry in the world. . . . For who will take paines for that which when he hath gotten it is not to be his owne, but must equally be shared in by every lazy, simple, dronish sot?"[51] True, he was not insensible to economic grievances. Many, he observed, were living in "great pompe," while "thousands . . . have not a bit of bread to put in their mouths," and he complained of "the multitudes of those oppressions . . . that lie upon the poor Common People, who are as a prey to all sorts and kinds of men, that are in Authority and Office."[52] He demanded therefore that persons who possessed less than £30 should be exempt from all taxes. Among the taxes, excise came in for his special condemnation, because it "enriches the Usurers, and other Catterpillars of the Commonwealth . . . out of the bowells of labourers and poor people."[53] Such passages, however, are not very frequent in his voluminous writings. Moreover, the same individualism which animated his political convictions led him to believe that the best remedy for these economic evils lay in free trade unrestricted by state or monopolies. It is quite significant that in his own writings there are no general attacks on agricultural enclosures. When he took up the public defence of some tenants who believed that their rights had been infringed by an enclosure, he did not discuss the ethics of enclosures at all (which he would have hardly omitted to do, we may assume, if he had held strong opinions about it), but based his claim exclusively on the legal rights of his clients applicable only to this particular case.[54] It is equally important to remember that he evidently did not want to abolish the inequalities of rank and status; this radical champion of the people's rights proclaimed with pride: "I am the sonne of a gentleman, and my Friends are of rancke and quality," and during his second trial in 1653 he raised an objection against his judge because of the latter's social inferiority.[55] Lilburne's conception of equality—this conclusion is inevitable—was limited by being purely political.

In calling Lilburne an individualist we must, of course, be particularly careful to distinguish his ideas from some of their later counterparts. Unlike the extreme individualists of a subsequent age, Lilburne did not neglect the small social unit. All mankind, he wrote, "raignes and governs as much by God in

D

their inferior orbs (of City, hundreds, wepentacks, and families) . . . as Kings in their Kingdoms."[56] We have noted above that he extolled the autonomous local community of Saxon times and that he suggested the transfer of all jurisdiction to local juries. Moreover, he wanted to abolish the offices, not only of permanent judges, but of all permanent magistrates; all public appointments, he demanded, should be filled by annual elections.[57] Such proposals presuppose that the centre of gravity lies in the local communities whose members know each other; they are unworkable when large numbers and anonymous social relations are involved. Lilburne's attitude can, indeed, be regarded as a protest against the growing tendency towards centralisation in the sixteenth and seventeenth centuries. One should not assume, at any rate, that his mental picture of society was identical with the fully developed modern state.

Nevertheless, the affinity of Lilburne's main ideas with a later climate of opinion is unmistakable. It is significant that his Puritan convictions did not prevent him from bestowing high praise on the founder of secular political science, Machiavelli, whom he called "one of the most wisest [sic] judicious and true lovers of his country of Italies liberties and freedomes, and generally of the good of all mankind that ever I read of in my daies."[58] Lilburne was evidently able to discover, behind a cloud of misunderstanding and abuse, the undeniable democratic tendencies in Machiavelli; in addition, Machiavelli's single-minded pursuit of political problems may well have impressed this ardent politician. Like many later reformers, Lilburne seems to have thought of justice mainly in political terms: his panaceas were parliamentary reform and constitutional laws (his legal turn of mind is quite typical). "Our former oppressions, and not-yet-ended troubles," he wrote in 1648, "have been occasioned either by want of frequent national meetings in council, or by the undue or unequal constitution thereof, or by rendering those meetings ineffectual."[59] In the future, men would increasingly concentrate on these issues and thus bring about an artificial separation of politics from all other sides of man's social life.

Lilburne's share in this general development would be of small account if it were not for the fact, repeatedly stressed above, that he was a representative Puritan of the Civil War period. He exemplifies the general statement that the main current of Puritanism was open to the influences of secularisation. His religion found its expression in an intense personal relationship to God, while the social elements of Christianity receded far into the background. His religious beliefs did, indeed, provide him with a firm basis for the equality of all the children of Adam, but when it came to building a society out of these equal individuals he relied on secular ideas. It has been suggested that Puritanism was particularly conducive to the growth of modern society in its early stages. The political thought of the Puritan John Lilburne is an important case in point.

How "Free-born John" came to doubt the value of his own political activities and ideas we do not know exactly. We only know that in the seclusion of his prison he experienced "a silent, still, quiet, home-dwelling, patient waiting upon God"; "divers hours in several nights," he wrote, ". . . my God denied sleep unto my outward eyes and caused my soul to be awake with himselfe." Now he regretted the time lost by his "former busling actings in the world" and his "Pen-contests and controversies." His troubled mind was to be set at rest by the new spiritual message of Quakerism, which he got to know through the books of James Nayler, William Dewsbury and Richard Hubberthorne. The one thing needful, he proclaimed, was to follow "the light of Christ shining in the soul," but this was infinitely harder than he had imagined. He was now overwhelmingly conscious of living in a fallen world whose laws were utterly opposed to the laws of Christ's kingdom; whatever was highly esteemed by the world was an "abomination in the sight of God." This cleavage went right through man's heart where the power of sin was raging. Unless man was inwardly cleansed and sanctified all attempts to establish the Kingdom of God would be of no avail and would lead to unending outward war in the world. Lilburne could, therefore, sincerely promise never to use violence of any kind. Henceforth his call would be for repentance and spiritual rebirth, addressed to the community of those who "are to love their enemies, to do good unto their haters, and to . . . requite their evill with good"; those who, in anticipation of the future kingdom of justice and peace, had beaten their swords into ploughshares and were joined together in mutual love.[60] This tone of Christian love had been entirely absent from Lilburne's earlier writings; he was now a new man. It is well to remember that these were the last words of one who was among the heralds of modern radical democracy.

Two of the men who, at one time or another, were associated with Lilburne in the leadership of the Leveller movement may be briefly considered here: Richard Overton and John Wildman.[61] Richard Overton's career was closely bound up with Lilburne's in the years between 1646 and 1649; he fought for the same causes and consequently found himself sometimes in the same prison. Some of his early years (it is unknown where and when he was born) he spent in Holland where he joined a congregation of non-Calvinistic Baptists. In England he became a professional pamphleteer and something of an unlicensed printer as well. Among his first tracts were vigorous attacks on religious persecution which he published under the pseudonym "Martin Mar-Priest," thus reviving the memory of the Puritan "Martin-Marprelate" controversy during the reign of Elizabeth. The best of these, *The Arraignement of Mr. Persecution*, is a lively allegory in the style of Bunyan. Overton, unlike Lilburne, was evidently interested in theological and philosophical speculation, and in 1644 he published a book called *Man's Mortallitie Or A Treatise Wherein 'tis proved . . . that Man . . . is a Compound wholly mortall.* There is, however, no connection between Overton's metaphysical speculations and his political views.[62] Later, Overton increasingly participated in Leveller politics; his pamphlets were mainly devoted to the spreading of Leveller principles and to the support of Leveller petitions. On most political issues Overton shared Lilburne's views. His statements on the law of nature, the equality of all men since

Adam, the sovereignty of the people, the "just old law of the land," and his quotations from Sir Edward Coke—all these could come from Lilburne's pamphlets. He was, however, more interested than Lilburne in the question of economic justice. He demanded that "all the grounds which anciently lay in common for the poor, and are now . . . enclosed" should be opened again, and that "all ancient charitable donations towards the constant relief of the poor . . . and all hospitals that are . . . vitiated from their primitive constitution" should be restored to the poor. This, together with the restoration and extension of free schools also suggested by him, would have done much towards mitigating the injustices caused by the economic upheavals of the sixteenth century. "Now is the time," he wrote, "for the compassionate Samaritan to appear . . .; for greater love and mercy cannot be amongst men than to take compassion over the helpless and destitute."[63]

John Wildman was a completely different type of man. According to Clarendon he was "bred a scholar in the university of Cambridge," but his name does not appear in the university registers. His contact with the Levellers may have originated in the army, of which he was a member some time before the autumn of 1647. In the winter of 1647-8 he organised the activities of the Levellers, in close association with Lilburne, but in the course of the following winter he severed his connections with them. From his long subsequent career as a land-speculator and conspirator (culminating after endless intrigues and counter-intrigues in the office of Postmaster-General, which he lost again for suspected tampering with letters) one derives the impression that he was one of those ambitious adventurers so common in revolutionary periods. Perhaps one might, with the necessary reservations, call him a republican: he was, at various times, in touch with Henry Marten and Algernon Sidney, and a member of James Harrington's Rota Club.[64] An unquestionably brilliant debater, he was chosen by the Army Levellers to plead their cause in the Army Council debates at Putney. Unlike the other Leveller leaders, Wildman does not seem to have had any connection with the sectarian movements so prominently represented in the New Model Army; he may well have had a share in strengthening Lilburne's secular tendencies. At Putney Wildman felt obviously ill at ease among so many people who were constantly invoking the Spirit of God. "I desire," he said, "as much as is possible to reverence whatsoever hath the Spirit or Image of God upon it," but he went on to make the bold statement that in politics it was extremely difficult to decide what the Spirit was actually saying because "we cannot find anything in the word of God [of] what is fit to be done in civil matters." For the rest, he took his stand on political liberty and equality. "Every person in England," he declared, "hath as clear a right to elect his representative as the greatest person in England."[65] On the important subject raised by Ireton—whether universal suffrage would endanger private property—Wildman remained silent. There is no reason whatever to suppose that he was greatly interested in questions of social justice.

Lilburne, Overton and Wildman were all, to some extent, in the public eye; many people knew that they took a leading part in Leveller affairs. Some observers, however, believed that another man directed the Levellers from the background, and it so happens that this was a very interesting man.

NOTES TO CHAPTER TWO

[Quotations in this chapter are from Lilburne's works unless stated otherwise.]

1 P. E. Gregg, *John Lilburne and the Leveller Movement* (Ph.D. Thesis, University of London, 1939) contains an interesting genealogical account of the Lilburne family. For all biographical details cf. C. H. Firth's article in the *D.N.B.*

2 The date of Lilburne's birth is uncertain; it lies somewhere between 1614 and 1618 (cf. P. E. Gregg, op. cit., and C. H. Firth, loc. cit.).

3 C. H. Firth, loc. cit.

4 *A Letter sent from Captaine Lilburne* (1643), pp. 4, 7.

5 *The Just Defence of John Lilburne, Against Such as charge him with Turbulency of Spirit* (1653), p. 9.

6 William Prynne, *The Lyar Confounded* (1645), p. 22; T. C. Pease, *The Leveller Movement* (1916), p. 328.

7 William Walwyn, *Walwyns Just Defence* (1649), p. 15.

[8] *The Selfe Afflicter Lively described in the whole course of the Life of Mr. John Lilburn* (1657), p. 2.

[9] Samuel Chidley, *The Dissembling Scot* (1653), p. 4.

[10] Anon., *A Declaration of some Proceedings of Lt.-Col. John Lilburn* (1648), p. 7. (This pamphlet contains the results of the investigations ordered by the House of Commons into the Leveller activities of the winter 1647–8.)

[11] *Lt.-Colonel John Lilburne, His Apologetical Narration* (Amsterdam, 1652), p. 59.

[12] C. H. Firth, loc. cit.

[13] *The Triall of Lieut.-Collonell John Lilburne* . . . Published by Theodorus Verax (1649), p. 151.

[14] *The Upright Man's Vindication* (1653), p. 15.

[15] *Just Defence*, pp. 2, 3.

[16] *The Legall Fundamentall Liberties of the People of England Revived, Asserted and Vindicated* (1649), pp. 19, 20. Lilburne's Puritanism was stressed again, after it had been forgotten for a long time, by W. Haller, in *The Rise of Puritanism* (1938).

[17] *Remarkable Passages in the Life of William Kiffin, Written by Himself, and edited by William Orme* (1823), p. 10.

[18] *A Worke of the Beast* (1638), pp. 4, 5, 8, 19.

[19] *The Resurrection of John Lilburne* (1656), pp. 6, 4.

[20] *An Answer to Nine Arguments* (written in 1638, published in 1645), p. 35.

[21] *Upright Man*, p. 1. (Cf. also: *Oppressed Mans Oppression declared* (1647,) p. 37; *The Picture of the Councel of State* (1649), p. 23; *Legall Fundamentall Liberties* (1649), p. 20; *Declaration to the Free-born People of England* (1652), p. 7.)

[22] *An Impeachment of High Treason Against Oliver Cromwel and his Son in Law Henry Ireton Esquires* (1649), p. 16.

[23] Lucy Hutchinson, *Memoirs of Colonel Hutchinson* (Everyman's edition), p. 64.

[24] *Apologetical Narration*, p. 5.

[25] *Jonahs Cry out of the Whales belly* (1647), p. 2.

[26] *Upright Man*, p. 15.

[27] *Impeachment*, pp. 15–16.

[28] Oliver Cromwell, Speech to First Protectorate Parliament, 4th September 1654.

[29] *A Discourse Betwixt Lieutenant Colonel John Lilburn, Close Prisoner in the Tower of London, and Mr. Hugh Peter* (1649), p. 4.

[30] *A Whip for the present House of Lords*, p. 23; *Discourse with Hugh Peter*, p. 6.

[31] *The Freeman's Freedom Vindicated* (1646), p. 12 (Woodhouse, *Puritanism and Liberty*, p. 318).

[32] *Upright Man*, pp. 13, 14.

[33] This turns up in the most unexpected places, as for instance in this piece of harmless doggerel verse:

> From the Norman Lawes and the French Guize,
> From a mercilesse creditor and a sudden surprize,
> Libera nos.

> (*Universal Madnesse, or, A new merry Letany* (1647), p. 5.)

For other examples, cf. M. James, *Social Problems*, and Woodhouse, op. cit.

[34] William Martyn, op. cit., p. 4.

[35] Quoted in Haller and Davies, *Leveller Tracts, 1647–1653*, Introduction, p. 46. Lilburne knew that book too.

[36] *Regall Tyrannie discovered* (1647), title-page, pp. 15, 86. In spite of Lilburne's denial, there can be little doubt that he was the author of this pamphlet.

[37] *Just Man's Justification* (1646), p. 14; *Oppressed Man's Oppression declared* (1647), p. 37. Cf. *Upright Man*, p. 12: "The known and declared fundamental laws . . . made by common consent in Parliament."

[38] *Just Man's Justification*, p. 13.

[39] Ibid., p. 15; *Whip for the House of Lords*, p. 13.

[40] *Regall Tyrannie*, p. 25.

[41] Ibid., pp. 16, 25 (cf. Samuel Daniel, *Complete Works*, ed. Grosart, 1896, iv, 165–6); Woodhouse, op. cit., p. 366. An interesting criticism of this proposal is contained in a pamphlet written by an anonymous supporter of the Agreement of the People: "In case the matter be depending between the Lord of the Mannour . . . and another private person, . . . how then is it possible for Justice to be truly and impartially distributed?" (*The Representative of Divers well-affected persons in and about the City of London* (1649), p. 9).

[42] *Regall Tyrannie*, p. 11.

[43] *Legall Fundamentall Liberties*, p. 22 and *passim*.

[44] *Innocency and Truth Justified* (1645), p. 52.

[45] *A Whip for the House of Lords* (1648), p. 17.

[46] *Freeman's Freedom*, pp. 11–12 (Woodhouse, op. cit., pp. 317–18).

[47] Ibid., p. 12 (Woodhouse, op. cit., p. 318).

[48] In 1647 the Levellers seem to have propagated unqualified manhood suffrage. In 1648 they proposed to exclude "persons receiving alms" and those who were "servants to, or receiving wages from, any particular person" (Woodhouse, op. cit., p. 357). This limitation was probably due to the fear that many of these people would have been semi-feudal retainers and therefore likely to have Royalist sympathies. In view of the Leveller theory it can be assumed that these restrictions were intended to be merely temporary.

[49] Cf. Ireton during the Putney debates.

[50] For the Diggers, cf. Chapter Six.

[51] *Apologeticall Narration*, pp. 68–9.

[52] *The Copy of a Letter from Lieutenant Colonell John Lilburne, to a friend* (1643), p. 16.

[53] *The second Part of England's New Chaines Discovered* (1649), p. 15.

[54] *The Case of the Tenants of the Mannor of Epworth* (1651).

[55] *Worke of the Beast*, p. 20; Pease, *The Leveller Movement*, p. 87.

[56] *Regall Tyrannie*, p. 40.

[57] *England's Birthright Justified* (1645), p. 48.

[58] *Upright Man*, p. 7. He did not express this view until 1653, so there can be no question of Machiavelli's influence on his earlier thought. In earlier pamphlets of his there are, in fact, the usual references to Machiavellianism as a term of abuse.

[59] *Foundations of Freedom*, Preamble to the Second Agreement of the People (1648), printed in Woodhouse, op. cit., p. 356.

[60] *The Resurrection of John Lilburne* (1656), pp. 18, 3, 9, 4, 11, 10, 12.

[61] Cf. *D.N.B.*, and W. Haller, *Tracts on Liberty*, vol. i. Very little is known about Thomas Prince, a wholesale trader in victuals, who shared the imprisonment of the Leveller leaders in 1649.

[62] For an interpretation of Overton's philosophy, see Appendix A.

[63] R. Overton, *Certain Articles for the Good of the Commonwealth* (1647): Woodhouse, op. cit., pp. 338, 337; R. Overton, *An Appeal from the Commons to the Free People* (1647): Woodhouse, op. cit., p. 331.

[64] An anonymous publication of 1659, called *The Leveller*, contains distinctly Harringtonian ideas and may well have been written by Wildman. This piece of intellectual borrowing without reference to the original source was noticed and unfavourably commented on by Harrington: *Works* (1771), p. 404.

[65] Woodhouse, op. cit., pp. 108, 66.

CHAPTER THREE

WILLIAM WALWYN: THE POWER OF LOVE

AMONG the radicals of the Puritan Revolution moved an enigmatic figure: the London merchant and Leveller, William Walwyn. Contemporary accounts of him run into extremes of praise and blame. His enemies held him responsible for all the Levellers' alleged intentions against property and order, and denounced him as a most dangerous underminer of all religion. An anonymous pamphleteer compared him to Thomas Münzer, "that Arch-Anabaptist," and Edwards, the author of *Gangraena*, called him a "dangerous man, a stronghead."[1] John Lilburne, on the other hand, referred to him as his "choicest comrade and fellow-sufferer" and as a man "as able in parts, as any is in England," and Walwyn's son-in-law, the physician Dr. Humphrey Brooke, praised the "Innocency and reall Goodnesse that is so visible in his life and conversation."[2] Some modern historians have shown great interest in Walwyn, especially in his radical views on social problems. T. C. Pease believes that "his part in the Leveller movement is easier underestimated than overestimated." He regards him, together with other Levellers, as a forerunner of the Liberal Democrats and Rationalists of later days, and therefore as "strangely modern" against the background of his age.[3] This view is substantially shared by W. Haller who calls Walwyn one of "the first great democrats of modern times," and by A. S. P. Woodhouse.[4] In view therefore of the interest which Walwyn has been able to arouse both among contemporaries and later historians,[5] it may be worth while to inquire what manner of man he was. Perhaps we can discover on what grounds he based his social criticism—what, in fact, was in his mind while he was making his short appearance on the political stage.

41

He was born in 1600, the second son of a Worcestershire country gentleman and the grandson of a bishop of Hereford.[6] He was sent to London and apprenticed to a silkman in Paternoster Row; in due course he became a member of the Merchant Adventurers' Company and was able to maintain a large family "from the profits of his Trade . . . in a middle and moderate but contentful condition."[7] In the Civil War he took the side of Parliament against what he thought to be "arbitrary power"; in November 1642 he became a member of a sub-committee of the City of London charged with the carrying out of a Parliamentary Ordinance "concerning the advancing of a considerable number of soldiers . . . and Armes."[8] To him, as to so many of his contemporaries, the Long Parliament, "under God the hope of the oppressed," seemed to usher in a new age and to foreshadow the removal of all grievances.[9] Quite early (probably in 1642) he put forward "certain infallible maximes of free Government: wherein the power of Parliament was plainly distinguished from the Kings Office, so plainly, that had it taken effect few men after due consideration thereof, would through error of judgement have taken part against the Parliament, or have befriended arbitrary power, as too many did for want of light."[10] In 1644 he believed Parliament to be "most ingenuous and impartiall of all others";[11] in 1646 he still declared that "God hath blessed all their undertakings in a wonderfull manner";[12] and in 1647 he petitioned Parliament "so effectually to fulfill the true ends of Parliaments in delivering this Nation, from these, and all other grievances, that none may presume or dare to introduce the like for ever."[13] In 1645, however, he had struck the first note of disillusionment. He praised the "exterpation of Episcopacie" and the "abolishing the High-Commission and Starre Chamber" as having been "no small matters," but he believed that "if the people be not totally freed from oppression of the same nature, they have a very small benefit"[14] from these measures. He now complained of the "Negligence, corruption, and unfaithfulnesse of Parliaments." "Looking upon the present [Government]," he wrote, "I still find a necessity of . . . my accustomed watchfullnesse, it never

being out of date."[15] From then onwards he seems to have
transferred his hopes more and more from Parliament to the
growing Leveller movement, which he probably joined in
1646.[16] By March 1647 he had become so prominent among
the Levellers that he drew up their petition which Parliament
ordered to be burnt by the hangman.[17] He also seems to have
had a share in the important liaison work between the London
Levellers and the Army Agitators.[18] When the Agreement of
the People was debated for the second time, in November 1648,
Walwyn was one of the four representatives of the Levellers
until one of the independents, who had "a prejudice against
him," forced his withdrawal.[19] In March 1649 he was sent to
the Tower together with Lilburne, Overton and Prince. The
charge brought against him (his suspected authorship of *England's New Chains Discovered*) was probably not justified, but it
seems that Cromwell was anxious to have the Leveller leaders
under lock and key in view of the army mutinies then threatening. After Lilburne's spectacular trial and acquittal Walwyn
was released too, in November 1649, and here his active par-
ticipation in politics seems to have practically come to an end.[20]
He may still have worked behind the scenes,[21] for as late as 1659
James Harrington included him among the members of a suggested committee which was to discuss Harrington's proposition for "a Commonwealth or Democracie."[22]

Although we have no account of Walwyn's education it is
clear from incidental references and from his writings generally
that he was exceptionally well-read. He seems to have been in
possession of a private library,[23] and he had accustomed himself
"to all kinds of good reading, and to the consideration of all
things." He also loved "an honest and discoursing Friend"; it
was, indeed, mainly to his Socratic powers of discussion that his
enemies ascribed his evil influence on other people.[24] Small
wonder, then, that this thoughtful and studious man came to
share the interest in religion so strongly prevailing at this time.
At some unknown date before 1640 he passed through a deep
spiritual crisis during which he was apparently in grave doubts
as to the possibility of his salvation. He gave the following

account of it in 1646: "Before this Parliament I was of full years to be sensible of the oppression of the times, being now forty five years of age; but so, as for a long time I took not boldnesse to judge, but upon the approbation of some authors and teachers that had captivated my understanding both in things morall, politique, and religious: in the last of which, being very serious and sincere in my application of things to my own conscience, my grounds being bad, though much applauded, I found much disconsolation therein, great uncertainty and at last extream affliction of mind, the Law and Gospel fighting for victory in me."[25] We catch another glimpse of this struggle in a pamphlet called *Walwin's Wiles*, in which some of Walwyn's former friends among the Baptists attacked him in 1649 while he was in prison: "Mr. Walwyn," reported the Baptists, "being asked by one of his intimate Friends . . . whether [the Scriptures] were the Word of God or No Replied thus . . . I believe it is not the Word of God, and I believe again it is the Word of God; . . . the Scripture is so plainly and directly contradictory to it self, that makes me believe it is not the Word of God; and yet again, all those passages therein that declare the nature of God, viz., his Grace and Goodness to men, I believe are the Word of God."[26]

Apart from this difficulty, Walwyn seems to have been further troubled by the obscurity of certain parts of the Bible; he maintained that "we must acknowledge that very many things [in the Scriptures] exceed our understandings."[27] Nor was he likely to get much help from the widely differing religious teachers of his time, whose impressive scholarship seemed to make confusion only worse confounded. He is said to have complained of the "contradictious opinions of men about matters of Religion, their various judgements, how opposite and cross they are to themselves, declining distinctions whereby they may be reconciled."[28] "At present," he wrote, "the World abounds with such variety of opinions concerning life and salvation, that many a sincere heart, seeking for peace and rest therein, is kept in perpetuall suspence and doubtfullnesse, whereby their lives become a very burthen to them; and many

sad and wofull effects follow thereupon."[29] Walwyn mentioned
a few of the theological writers to whom he might have turned
for help: Hooker, Perkins, Downham, Hall—Anglicans and
Puritans of various shades of opinion who disagreed, of course,
on many important points.[30]

But just as it had been the Bible which had caused this crisis
(and not, it should be stressed, any of the numerous other books
which Walwyn had read), so it was to be the Bible again which
would set his mind at rest. In this conflict between Law and
Gospel, "the Scriptures," he wrote, "were taken in more
singly, and void of glosse, to my assistance, by the cleare light
whereof I saw the enemies I feared vanquished, which wrought
a real thankfulnes in me towards Christ, which increased with
the increasings of faith."[31] It was probably Luther's problem
which had troubled him: how could a constant violator of God's
commandments be justified in His sight? He now arrived at an
Antinomian solution: the Old Testament had been invalidated
by the New, the Law had lost its force through Grace; and so,
he added, "my heart was at much more ease and freedom than
others."[32] He still believed that "by the deeds of the law shall
no flesh be justified in his sight: for by the law is the knowledge
of sinne"[33] (Romans iii, 20), but, he went on, "I am not a
preacher of the law but of the gospell; nor are you under the
law but under grace. . . . Yee are all justified freely by his
grace through the redemption that is in Jesus Christ"[34]
(Romans vi, 14; iii, 24).

With regard to the obscurity of many biblical passages, he
adopted the Latitudinarian practice of concentrating on the
clear and uncontroversial points: "My experience tell[s] me,"
he wrote, "that we have no bettering of our understanding, or
quieting of our mindes . . . from any places of Scripture that
hath any obscurity in them, but from such as are clearly exempt
from all difficulty. . . . God hath dealt abundantly well with us;
there being nothing that is necessary for the enlightning of our
understandings, or the peace of our mindes, but what hee hath
plainely declared and manifestly set forth in his word."[35]

Once his early spiritual crisis was overcome Walwyn held

fast to the solution at which he had arrived. The basis of his religious thought was his belief in the goodness of God and His love towards mankind. He expressed that in 1649 in a passage with which he opened his defence against the charge of atheism brought against him by the Baptists, a fine example of his balanced and beautiful prose: "From my serious and frequent consideration of the goodnesse of God towards man, the innumerable good things he created for his sustenance and comfort; that he hath made him of so large a capacity as to be Lord over other creatures; ever testifying his love, by giving rain and fruitfull seasons, feeding our hearts with food and gladnesse: That he hath made him, as his own Vicegerent, to see all things justly and equally done, and planted in him an ever-living conscience to mind him continually of his duty; I could not but wonder that this should not be sufficient to keep mankind in order and the world in quiet."[36] It was this wonderful love of God which caused Him to send His son Jesus Christ to save the world: "Had it not beene for this inexpressible and unexampled love, you had beene eternally wretched and miserable, companions of Devils, and damned spirits in Hell for ever, where the Worme never dieth, and the fire never goeth out."[37] Walwyn believed (following John's First Epistle) that "the same Jesus whom the Jewes crucified, was Lord and Christ: That he is the propitiation of our sins, and not only for ours, but for the sins of the whole world, that it is the blood of Christ which cleanseth us from all sinne, that his love is so exceeding towards us, that even when we were enemies, Christ dyed for us"[38] (1 John ii, 2; i, 7).

It is not surprising that Walwyn seemed to have found it difficult to square this belief in the goodness of God and in Jesus, who had taken away the sin of the world, with the doctrine of eternal damnation. His opponents maintained, and his son-in-law Humphrey Brooke admitted, that at one time Walwyn believed in universal redemption. He is supposed to have said: "Can it enter into your heart to conceive that God should cast a man into everlasting burnings where he should be tormented for ever without end, for a little time of sinning in this world?" He seems to have believed at that time "that all the hell that was, was only that which was in an ill man's conscience in this life."[39] This, however, he found to be untenable: Humphrey Brooke reported that "upon strict search which we together have made into the Scripture, we have concluded that there is another Hel succeeding judgment, convinced by those places of Scripture, Psal. vi, 8; Matt. xxv, 41; 2 Thess. 1 . . . And though it seems contrary to reason that a man should be punished everlastingly for a little sinning in this world, in which sense only he spoke it: yet have we both submitted our Reasons to God's Word, the places fore mentioned being expresse for the same."[40]

Having learnt the value of an independent inquiry in the search for truth, Walwyn became a generous advocate of religious liberty, although he was not himself a member of a sect and remained, like many Latitudinarians, in communion with his "parochial congregation."[41] It should not be forgotten that all his pamphlets before 1647 have religious toleration for their main theme. "Of all liberty," he maintained, "liberty of Conscience is the greatest: and where that is not a true Christian findeth none."[42] But this was not the only result of his newly found faith. He now felt "a real thankfulnes . . . towards Christ, which increased with the increasings of faith: insomuch as I set my self daily more and more to do his will: and that in a more publick way than formerly."[43] He evidently regarded his entry into politics as the carrying out of a religious duty. There was something, moreover, which he now felt an urge to proclaim: he had learnt to see the Gospel in a new light and he had thus rediscovered for himself certain aspects of the Christian religion which Protestantism in general and Puritanism in particular had tended to neglect.

Among these, the most outstanding was the teaching of what he called practical Christianity.[44] God's love and goodness towards mankind should, he thought, engender a similar love and goodness among men: "We should love as Christ hath loved, Who gave himself an Offering and a Sacrifice for us: so that if we would try each other's Faith, we are to consider each other's love; so much faith, so much love; so much love, so much pure and undefiled Religion."[45] On another occasion he wrote: "If you would be esteemed a disciple of Christ, it must be knowne by love,"[46] and then went on to quote at length from Paul's panegyric on Love (1 Cor. xiii).

How were Christians to show their love to one another? There was, he believed, no lack of opportunity. "He that hath this world's goods, and seeth his brother lack, how dwelleth the love of God in him? Judge then by this rule who are of God's family; looke about and you will finde in these woefull dayes thousands of miserable, distressed, starved, imprisoned Christians: see how pale and wan they looke: how coldly, raggedly, and unwholesomely they are cloathed. Live one weeke with them in their poore houses, lodge as they lodge, eate as they eate, and no oftener, and bee at the same passe to get that wretched food for a sickly wife and hunger-starved children (if you dare doe this for feare of death or diseases); then walke abroad, and observe the generall plenty of all necessaries, observe the gallant bravery of multitudes of men and women abounding in all things that can be imagined: observe likewise the innumerable numbers of those that have more than sufficeth."[47] It was the duty of Christians to relieve this poverty in the midst of plenty, and to "help the distressed and any waies afflicted" was the "intent and substantiall scope" of religion.[48] In enumerating the works of practical Christianity he followed, of course, mainly the Gospel catalogue of Matthew xxv, 35, but made characteristic additions. Christians, he thought, "should be imployed to feed the hungry, cloath the naked, or in visiting the fatherlesse and widdow, or in delivering the Captive, and setting the oppressed free, all which are workes so fully and plainly set forth in Scripture, as most pleasing to God."[49] The nearest scripture parallels to "delivering the Captive, and setting the oppressed free" are actually contained in Isaiah lviii, 6 and i, 17, and in Psalms lxxxii, 4, but it is clear that Walwyn considered these demands to be in perfect harmony with the spirit of the Gospel. He believed, indeed, that Christians could show their "universal love to all mankind" by "freeing a Commonwealth from all Tyrants, oppressors, and de-ceivers."[50]

Most of Walwyn's views on social and economic matters were derived from his conception of practical Christianity. In his imaginary sermon, *The Power of Love*, he answered the question: "Would you have all things common?" by a refer-ence to the communism of the Apostles (Acts ii, 44): "You may remember the multitude of believers had all things com-mon."[51] This practice of the early Christians was the effect of their "Charity and heavenly mindednesse, which the blessed Apostles begot in them." He added, however, that this arrange-ment among them had been "Voluntary, not Coactive"; it was not an obligation laid on all Christians and could, therefore, only be reintroduced by "universall assent thereunto from all and every one of the People."[52] Walwyn's enemies reported him as having said in private conversation "that it would never be well untill all things were common, and it being replyed, Will that ever be? [he] answered, We must endeavour it."[53] This may well represent his view fairly accurately: perhaps he thought communism a desirable aim and said so at times but did not regard it as being within the range of contemporary politics. It should be noted, too, that he never defended the institution of private property in the manner of John Lilburne.[57] It is therefore reasonable to assume that the official Leveller rejection of communism was mainly due to Lilburne's influence.

Walwyn was, at any rate, strongly opposed to inequality of wealth. He did not refute the charge brought against him that he was "very frequent and diligent in fomenting the considera-tion of the disproportion and inequality of the distribution of the things of this life. What an inequitable thing it is for one man to have thousands, and another want bread, and that the pleasure of God is, that all men should have enough, and not that one man should abound in this world's goods, spending it upon his lusts, and another man of far better deserts, not to be worth twopence."[55] This is also borne out by Walwyn's atti-tude to the specific social evils and the economic changes of his time. Usury seemed to him to be "contrary to all example of

E

the Apostles and first Christians," equivalent to a denial of God.[56] Hardly less important was the enclosure problem, concerning which he did not deny having said that "he could wish with all his heart that there was neither Pale, Hedg nor Ditch in the whole Nation."[57] As regards his attitude towards the poor we have already noticed his repeated emphasis on works of charity; accordingly he asked Parliament in his petition that they should "provide some powerful means to keep men, women and children from begging and wickedness, that this nation may be no longer a shame to Christianity therein."[58] On another work of charity, the relief of prisoners, all the Leveller leaders, having first-hand experience in this matter, were very outspoken. Demanding redress, Walwyn wrote: "Prison-keepers or gaolers are as presumptuous as ever they were both in receiving and detaining of prisoners illegally committed, [and are] as cruel and inhumane to all . . . as oppressive and extorting in their fees, and are attended with under-officers of such vile and unchristian demeanour as is most abominable." Finally, we should mention Walwyn's concern for the reform of criminal law, of the law of contract with regard to both debtors and creditors; in short, of all laws which, he boldly proclaimed, ought to be reduced "to the nearest agreement with Christianity."[59] An anonymous opponent of the 1647 petition drew particular attention to this phrase and ascribed to it a subtle meaning which would probably have eluded a modern reader. Behind the words "the *nearest* agreement" he saw lurking the doctrine of Christian anarchy: "as if Politicall Lawes could not quite agree . . . [with Christianity], or we be other than mongrill Christians while we retained any"—and in suggesting this he may not have been wide of the mark.[60]

We have said that the traditional social teaching of the Churches (to some extent corresponding to Walwyn's "practical Christianity") had tended to fall into neglect even amongst professing Christians. In England, as R. H. Tawney has shown, this was especially marked from the end of the sixteenth century onwards. Walwyn was fully aware of this change and its implications: "Time was," he said, "that it was otherwise in England . . .; but then Godlinesse was esteemed the greatest gain." "But our times, though we call them times of light, yet do abound with gluttony, usury, pride, oppression, and all kinds of wickednesse."[61] He was heard to insist "upon the unworthynesse of our times, in making riches and estates, and the things of this world, the great badge of distinction between man and man."[62] This was evidently opposed to the practice of Christ, for "were not the poor and unlearned Fishermen and Tentmakers . . . made choyce of for Christ's Disciples and Apostles?"[63] Moreover, it was not only the economic development and the acquisitive spirit of his time that Walwyn deplored. He maintained also that those of his contemporaries who regarded themselves, and were regarded by the world, as most religious, took a leading share in the growth of commercialism; he asserted, in fact, a connection between the spirit of Capitalism and Puritanism. The Independents, Walwyn found, in 1649 "are increased in numbers and have, as it were, scummed the Parish Congregations of most of their wealthy and zealous members"; "it seems," he told an Independent minister, "your Congregation is of a near relation to those that hold prosperity a mark of the true Church."[64] He attacked the Puritans for their unchristian business practices and lack of charity which compared unfavourably with those of non-Christians or Catholics. He was, so we are told, "ever and anon harping upon the hardheartednesse and uncharitablenesse of Professors . . . and those that are religious men, how grinding they are in bargains, how penurious, base and backward in works of charity and mercy, how undermining and overreaching they are in buying, in selling, how having and craving in the things of this life, . . . how they let their brethren starve, and dye, and perish, rather than help them, and how bountifull, free and liberall the very Heathens have been, and how beneficiall even Papists, and many that doe not so much as pretend to Religion, are to the Poore."[65] "Nay, so impudent are some of these proud boasting Churchers (who glory to follow precisely the pattern shewed in the [Sermon on the] mount) that contrary to all example of the Apostles and first Christians, they can content themselves to be known usurers, and those that are not such themselves, can allow it in their fellow-Members, their Pastors, Elders and Deacons can tolerate it."[66] The conclusion which Walwyn drew was bitter: "Observe them well, and you shall see Christ and Belial, God and Mammon in one and the same person: Christ in shew, the other in reality."[67]

Walwyn laid a great deal of responsibility for this state of affairs at the door of the ministers of religion whose interest it was, instead of promoting the common brotherhood of men, "to make themselves a peculiar Tribe of a nearer relation to God than other men." They were like the Pharisees of the Gospel; they "love to sit uppermost at feasts, and to be reverenced in publicke places."[68] In order to keep and increase their dominion they had "in processe of time . . . confounded . . . the cleare streames of the Scripture, and perverted the true Gospel of Jesus Christ, and by politicke Glosses and Comments introduced an other Gospell sutable to the covetous, ambitious, and persecuting spirit of the Clergie. . . . They then began to scorne the simplicity and meannesse of the Apostles . . . and to engrosse great Livings, Lordships, Territories and Dominions."[69] Or, as Dr. Brooke put it, "upon the plain and innocent basis of the Christian Religion, instituted by him who thought fit to appear in the World as the Son of a Carpenter . . . hath been erected . . . a stately Scene of external pomp and splendor."[70] If one wanted to be a "substantial Christian" one had to penetrate, beyond all these accretions, to the Scriptures, "the only true infallible teacher of spirituall things in our time";[71] everything that was necessary for salvation was contained in God's Word.

This Christian Primitivism is of course, in one form or another, a common feature of Protestant thought, but in Walwyn's case it was linked with a wider Primitivism derived from ancient and Renaissance sources, especially from Seneca, Lucian and Montaigne.[72] It is this, in fact, which constitutes the second main element of Walwyn's thought.

As a measuring-rod for the social reality around him he used not only the ethics of Christianity but also the classical conception of the state of nature when man, "judging rightly of all things, and desiring only what was necessary, and so being exempt from all labour, and care of obtaining things super-fluous, . . . passed his dayes with aboundance of delight and contentment."[73] The traditional description of this state of nature included communal ownership and the absence of law and government; communism and anarchy were, indeed, among its outstanding features.[74] It is more than likely that Walwyn was led to accept communism in this way too, especially as Dr. Brooke, who faithfully echoed Walwyn on most points, mentioned explicitly that "in the world's infancy and innocency, there was no need of any reserves, every man's breast was and might safely be open to all: till propriety . . . made us all draw several wayes, and every man labour to fill his own Barn."[75] The problem of anarchy was raised by Walwyn's supposed answer to a suggestion that communism would destroy all government. He is reported to have said that once communism was adopted "there would be less need of Government, for then there would be no theeves, no covetous persons, no deceiving and abusing of one another. . . . But if in such a case they have a form and rule of government to determine cases, as may fall out, yet there will be no need of standing Officers in a Common Wealth. . . . Take a Cobler from his Seat, or a butcher from his Shop, . . . and let him heare the case, and determine the same, and then betake himself to his work again."[76] It seems that this conception underlies the characteristic Leveller demand for annual local juries to decide all judicial cases arising in a particular district to the exclusion of all professional officials or lawyers.[44] In Walwyn's mind this idea may have received additional support from his tendency towards Christian anarchy: nothing, he thought, was more unchristian than "mastery," and he reminded his readers of Christ's injunction to his followers that they should not "propose dominion and the sway over . . . their Brethren."[78]

In establishing this state of nature God had shown His love to mankind no less than in revealing the Scriptures, and Walwyn, as we have seen, asked himself why this should not have been "sufficient to keep mankind in order and the world in quiet."[79] The answer was grave but clear: the world had fallen from its state of integrity and the consequences were necessarily disastrous.[80] Man lost his original state when he "sought out unto himself many inventions . . . of superfluous subtilities and artificiall things, which have been multiplied with the ages of the world." Now everything has become "totally corrupted: our first instructions, and all after discourses have beene indulgent flatterers to our darling superfluities."[81] Here again it would be impossible to separate the secular from the religious: the "superfluities," seen from another angle, were the "unnecessary cares that choake the Word" (Matt. xiii, 22);[82] the world was opposed both to a natural life and to the Word; in Walwyn's mind the state of nature and the *status innocentiae*, Golden Age and Paradise, seem to have merged into one.

It would be a mistake to regard Walwyn's reference to the Golden Age as merely a literary echo. Together with Christian ethics it enabled him to see the things around him more sharply and it was in its turn reinforced by acute observation. Most men, he found, were "engaged in one kind of corrupt interest or other" and were "meere worldlings."[33] He rarely failed to compare clergymen to those silversmiths of Ephesus who cried, "Great is Diana of the Ephesians," lest they should lose their trade.[84] He expressed the belief—widespread after more than a century of religious wars—that they, more than any other class of men, were "the Troublers of the World. . . . They embroyle States in warres . . . and divert the people from the prosecution of their owne interest, (which is their safety and libertie) to maintaine their quarrells."[85] All their theological subtleties were entirely superfluous and used by them only to make men believe that the necessary doctrines were hard to understand.[86] University men generally he accused of using their learning "as an Art to deceive and abuse the understandings of men."[87] Politicians came in for his angry contempt; they were "Satan's chief Agents" and were necessarily bound up with corrupt interests, "for a just course of life . . . needs no crafts or policies to support it."[88] In May 1649 he compiled an extensive catalogue of those who, dressed in a little brief authority, were opposing the Levellers and pursuing unnatural aims under the corrupting influence of power: "Either he hath two or three offices or trusts upon him, by which he is enriched and made powerfull; or he hath an office in the excise, or customs; or is of some monopolising company; or interested in the corruption of the laws; or is an encloser of fens, or other commons, or hath charge of publique monies in his hands, for which he would not willingly be accomptable; or hath kept some trust, authority or command in hand longer than commission and time intended; or being in power, hath done something that cannot well be answered; or that hath money upon usury in the excise; or that makes title of tythes, and the like burthenous grievances; or else such as have changed their principles with their condition, and of pleaders for liberty of Conscience, whilst they were under restraint, . . . [have] now become persecutors, so soon as they are freed from disturbance; or some that have been projectors, still fearing an after-reckoning; or that have received gifts, or purchased the publicke lands at under-values."[89]

We have quoted this passage at such length to show how comprehensive was Walwyn's suspicion of the "most active, prosperous and successful persons of the Nation,"[90] and how keen was his insight into contemporary affairs. Whatever view one may take of the men whom Walwyn attacked, it is certain that they were the principal sharers in the benefits of the Puritan Revolution. This, he thought, was unjust also in view of the fact that "the great things that have been done for the Parliament, have been done by the meaner sort of men."[91] So far from advancing the rich, a Commonwealth ought to use "all friendliness . . . towards *the meanest of the people especially*"[92] (Walwyn's italics).

Enough has been said to illustrate Walwyn's radical criticism of contemporary society. He was, however, like some other primitivists, quite hopeful of mankind's ability to regain the state of nature. Natural things were, after all, "ready at hand, or easily to be had." They were, moreover, "to be understood easily without study," and God had made man "naturally a rational creature" so that he should be able to grasp them.[93] (Here it becomes obvious, by the way, that Walwyn's conception of reason was closely bound up with his primitivism: it was a remnant of man's unfallen state, not a result of his progressive development.[94]) It was because of natural reason that even the "very heathen and meere naturall men" arrived at a true idea of a life *secundum naturam*.[95] But a Christian was helped in other ways as well to see the light. In addition to his conscience planted in him by God, he could rely on the Gospel which was "so sweet and delectable as cannot but be embraced, so certain as cannot be doubted, so powerfull to dissolve man into love."[96] Its necessary doctrines were few and could be easily taught "by conferences and mutuall debates," and by God's grace the "meanest capacity" was fully capable of understanding them. If men would only free themselves from their "Church-bondage," they would by reading the Scriptures soon become "substantial Christians" and *"fall to practice"*[97] (Walwyn's italics). Walwyn was, in fact, like so many of his contemporaries, a believer in the approach of the Millennium. He did not, indeed, anticipate the Second Coming of Christ, but he did expect the rule of practical Christianity on earth. Christian love in conjunction with human reason, so his equable temperament and the events of the 1640's made him believe, would heal the world's corruption.

These wider hopes did not prevent him, of course, from sharing many of the political doctrines of the other Levellers. He too believed that any power Parliament had was entrusted to it by the people and that, if this trust was broken, the people were entitled to resume their power and to establish their fundamental rights by concluding an agreement among themselves.[98] Like other Levellers, especially John Lilburne, he was certain "that true Christians are of all men the most valiant defenders of the just liberties of their Country."[99] But it should be noted that Walwyn hardly ever appealed to Magna Carta, to the supposed Anglo-Saxon liberties or to the law of nature. Bearing in mind Walwyn's thought as a whole we cannot but conclude that it outran the "Legall Fundamentall Liberties" and the Agreement of the People.

It is clear, then, that Walwyn derived his social radicalism mainly from two sources: from his interpretation of the Gospel and from classical primitivism. As to the latter, its tradition in England and its strength in the seventeenth century are still insufficiently explored. It could probably be shown that it underlies a good deal of social thought bound up with a certain conception of "nature" (as implied, for example, in More's *Utopia*). In reading Seneca, Lucian and Montaigne, Walwyn was, of course, sharing a widespread contemporary taste. With regard to his practical Christianity the line of tradition is clearer. He could rely on widely accepted ideas embodied, for example, in the works of the Tudor preachers and moralists and their seventeenth-century successors. Condemnation of usury and enclosures, concern for the relief of the poor, emphasis on the works of Christian charity and profound suspicion of the growing commercialism, were all contained in the works of these writers who based themselves largely on the social teaching of the medieval Church. With even more justification can we regard Walwyn as the heir of the Christian sect tradition with its bitter attacks on the clergy, its claims of Christian equality and its denunciation of the unbrotherly social institutions of this world. This tradition may have reached him in various ways. He knew a good deal about the German Anabaptists of the sixteenth century and professed not to believe the books which had been written to discredit them.[100] He was also well acquainted with the sectarians of his own time, among whom these ideas were reappearing during the 1640's. And it should not be forgotten that this Christian radicalism has its firm roots in the Gospel; Walwyn clearly belonged to the long and distinguished line of those who had protested against the Christian compromise with the world and, latterly, against the growth of the "acquisitive society."

The reference to the sectarian tradition is relevant for yet another reason. Ernst Troeltsch has suggested that the medieval sects owed their picture of the Millennium to the stoic doctrine of the state of nature which had been introduced into Christian thought by the early Fathers.[101] Whether Troeltsch is right or not (and his theory is still the subject of controversy), in Walwyn's case, at any rate, this combination takes place under our very eyes. It is an interesting example of a recurring feature of our history: of the successful blending of classical and Christian elements (to which Renaissance influences lent themselves more readily than some of their interpreters would lead one to believe).

All this complex background has to be borne in mind in discussing Walwyn as a "forerunner" of later movements. He was an early democrat, communist or rationalist only to the limited extent that these later currents of thought owed something to earlier ideas. Their whole background, however (the secularised world of the Enlightenment and the nineteenth century), is altogether so different from Walwyn's that it seems hardly justifiable to establish such a direct relationship. But one could perhaps argue that the free religious inquiry of men like Walwyn, which inevitably resulted in a weakening of dogma, and their extreme anticlericalism may have ultimately hindered the resistance of Christianity against that complete secularisation of which we are the bewildered heirs. On this point more will be said later.

Walwyn must have witnessed the rapid passing away of the age to which he belonged: he died as late as 1680 at the age of eighty. He did not, however, end his days as a merchant. It may be conjectured that the Merchant Adventurers retaliated in some way or other against a man who had asked Parliament to dissolve their "oppressive company."[102] However that may be, Walwyn became what he chose to call "a physician" and what amounted in practice to being an apothecary; he may have been helped in this by his son-in-law, Dr. Brooke, who eventually became a Fellow of the Royal College of Physicians in London. Walwyn advertised the principles guiding him in his new calling and the effectiveness of his medicines in a book called *Physick for Families* (published posthumously, and perhaps commemoratively, in 1681). We recognise some of his old views in his statement that he relied on his medicines "solely from their powerfull friendliness to Humane Nature," strongly deprecating such "artificial" procedures as blood-letting or purging.[103] In this book he mentioned that he had tried some of his own remedies during the "last great Mortality" (p. 144); if, as seems probable, this refers to the Great Plague of 1665, then he must already have adopted his new profession by that date. His last will suggests that in his later days he must have been fairly well off: he made four bequests of £200 each, and left the rest to a son-in-law to whom he had also "Communicated all his Secrets."[104]

Here we must leave William Walwyn, not without regret. His life in his private circle, probably uneventful, has left no traces behind. It is a pity that we cannot re-create it: we may feel that the destiny of man is better served by his like than by the "men of destiny." Our impression of him, despite the limitation of our sources, is surprisingly definite. His outward appearance, known to us from an engraving showing him in old age, reveals the keen intelligence of his eyes and the gentle friendliness of his face. Having read his writings one feels to have been in contact with "an honest and discoursing Friend": the very tone of his voice is still audible behind the printed word. It was a quiet voice, more at home in intimate conversation than in public oratory, creating confidence, evoking sympathy, commanding respect. His manner, even in attack, was urbane; not even in prison did he lose his sense of proportion. He was a civilised man, and therefore he never forgot the shortcomings of his civilisation; although he was intensely interested in the issues of his age, he was always able to look at them with detachment. There was in him a certain serenity springing from the possession and exercise of a virtue which he never ceased to extol, and without which we are "as sounding brass or a tinkling cymbal."

NOTES TO CHAPTER THREE

[Unless stated expressly, works quoted in this chapter are by Walwyn.]

[1] W. Kiffin, and others, *Walwins Wiles* (1649); Anon., *Some observations on the late dangerous petition* (19th Sept. 1648), p. 25; T. Edwards, *Gangraena* (1646), i, 96.

[2] Lilburne, *Legall Fundamentall Liberties* (1649), p. 20; Lilburne, *Apologeticall Narration* (1652), p. 13; H. B. Med (= Humphrey, not Henry, Brooke), *Charity of Churchmen* (1649), p. 1. For Brooke, cf. *D.N.B.*; for his family relation to Walwyn, Brooke, *The Durable Legacy* (1681), p. 115.

[3] T. C. Pease, *The Leveller Movement* (1916), pp. 253, 217.

[4] Haller, *Tracts on Liberty*, i, 28; Woodhouse, *Puritanism and Liberty*, Introduction, p. 55.

[5] W. K. Jordan calls him "one of the most interesting and stimulating of the numerous lay thinkers of the age" (*The Development of Religious Toleration*, iv (1940), 181).

[6] Cf. the pedigree and the coat of arms of his family in *Visitation of the County of Worcester 1682–83* (ed. W. C. Metcalfe, Exeter, 1803), p. 100. (Mr. G. Parsloe, of the Institute of Historical Research, kindly drew my attention to this pedigree.) His eldest brother Herbert, who became a M.A. of Lincoln College, Oxford, was described as "armiger" in the University Register (Foster, *Alumni Oxonienses*). Walwyn's father, it was stated, was worth £300–400 p.a. (Brooke, *Charity*, p. 10).

[7] Brooke, *Charity*, pp. 10, 11.

[8] Husband's *Collection*, p. 753 (quoted in *Notes and Queries*, 9th ser., iv, 163).

[9] *Petition* (1647), p. 2. A list of Walwyn's writings will be found in Haller, *Tracts on English Liberty*, i, 120. Most of Walwyn's writings are now easily accessible in Haller, op. cit., and Haller and Davies, *Leveller Tracts 1647–1653* (1944).

[10] *A Whisper in the Eare of Mr. T. Edwards* (1646), p. 3. I have not been able to identify these proposals.

[11] *The Compassionate Samaritane* (1644), p. 77. Haller's ascription can, I think, safely be followed.

[12] *A Word more to Mr. T. Edwards* (1646), p. 4.

[13] *Petition* (1647), p. 7.

[14] *England's Lamentable Slaverie* (1645), p. 5. I have followed T. C. Pease's suggestion that this pamphlet was written by Walwyn.

[15] *Slaverie*, title-page, p. 2.

[16] Cf. Haller, op. cit., i.

[17] For Walwyn's authorship, see Haller, i, 116.

[18] Brooke, *Charity*, p. 10; *Fountain*, p. 17.

[19] Woodhouse, op cit., p. 343.

[20] Apart from a pamphlet vindicating juries against Henry Robinson's attacks (1651), and a memorandum directed against the Levant Company (1652); cf. M. James, *Social Problems*, pp. 155–7.

[21] Perhaps even in his native county: there was a group of "Levellers" in Worcestershire as late as the 1670's (*Victoria County History: Worcester*, iv, 192, 456. I am indebted for this reference to Dr. R. H. Tawney).

[22] James Harrington, *A Proposition in order to the Proposing of a Commonwealth or Democracie* (1659). The account of Walwyn in the *D.N.B.* ends in 1651.

23 Kiffin, *Wiles*, p. 9.

24 *Whisper*, p. 3; *Fountain*, p. 22; Kiffin, *Wiles*, *passim*.

25 *Whisper*, p. 3.

26 Kiffin, *Wiles*, p. 10.

27 *The Vanitie of the Present Churches* (1649), p. 33. Haller regards this as one of Walwyn's pamphlets and this is likely to be the case. For our purpose it is sufficient that Walwyn agreed with its contents: "I might enlarge my self upon this theme, but the little book, called, the vanity of the present churches, hath prevented me, unto which I refer the ingenious reader" (*Just Defence*, p. 23).

28 Kiffin, *Wiles*, p. 8.

29 *Vanitie*, p. 13.

30 Walwyn's *Just Defence* (1649) (quoted by Haller, op. cit., i, 39).

31 *Whisper*, p. 3.

32 Walwyn's *Just Defence*, p. 3 (quoted by Haller, op. cit., i, 38).

33 *The Power of Love* (1643), p. 21. There can be little doubt that Haller's ascription of this tract to Walwyn is correct.

34 *Love*, pp. 20, 24.

35 Ibid., pp. 10, 7.

36 *Fountain*, p. 1.

37 *Love*, p. 34.

38 *Vanitie*, p. 30 (Walwyn quotes "God is love," 1 John iv, 8, in *Love*, Preface, and *Word*, pp. 4–5).

39 Kiffin, *Wiles*, p. 10.

40 Brooke, *Charity*, p. 4.

41 *Whisper*, p. 5; Brooke, *Charity*, p. 11.

42 *A Word More*, p. 5.

43 *Whisper*, p. 3.

44 *Fountain*, p. 1.

45 *Vanitie*, p. 30.

46 *Whisper*, p. 9.

47 *Love*, Preface.

48 *Vanitie*, p. 43.

49 Ibid., p. 23.

50 Ibid., p. 43.

51 *Love*, Preface.

52 Lilburne, Walwyn, Prince and Overton, *A Manifestation of those unjustly styled Levellers* (1649). (The authors of *Walwins Wiles* believed that the *Manifestation* was written by Walwyn alone, and Dr. Brooke seems to have shared this view.)

53 Kiffin, *Wiles*, p. 13. Walwyn's apologist, Dr. Brooke, had to admit that Walwyn had at times expressed communist views "in heat of Discourse": *Charity*, p. 2. Walwyn himself maintained that he was no more for "Levelling" than could be deduced from his petition of 1647 (*Fountain*, p. 7), and thus subtly evaded the issue, as this petition, unlike other Leveller documents, did not deal with the question at all. On another occasion, however, he claimed that his views on communism were contained in the Agreement of the People which expressly repudiates any communist tendencies (*Just Defence* (1649), p. 24).

54 Cf. Chapter Two of this study.

55 Kiffin, *Wiles*, p. 12.

56 *Vanities*, p. 25; *Fountain*, p. 5.

57 Kiffin, *Wiles*, p. 16.

58 *Petition* (1647), p. 6.

59 Ibid., Preface, pp. 5, 6.

60 Anon., *Some Observations*, p. 26. For supporting evidence concerning Christian Anarchy, cf. below.

61 *Vanitie*, p. 19; *Love*, p. 33.

62 Kiffin, *Wiles*, p. 14.

63 *Samaritane*, p. 33.

64 *Vanitie*, p. 11; *Just Defence*, p. 16.

65 Kiffin, *Wiles*, p. 13.

66 *Vanitie*, p. 25.

67 *Fountain*, p. 25.

68 *Samaritane*, pp. 27, 41.

69 *Vanitie*, pp. 33, 24.

70 Brooke, *The Durable Legacy* (1681), p. 39.

71 *Vanitie*, pp. 4, 42.

72 These authors are included in his reading list (quoted in Haller, op. cit., i, 39). He gives a clearly primitivistic reason for finding Lucian enjoyable: "for his good ends in discovering the vanity of things in worldly esteem" (Haller, ibid.).

73 *Love*, p. 3.

74 Cf. *Primitivism and Related Ideas in Antiquity* (ed. A. O. Lovejoy and G. Boas, 1935).

75 Brooke, *Legacy*, p. 137.

76 Kiffin, *Wiles*, p. 16.

77 Cf. the final Agreement of the People (published by Lilburne, Walwyn, Prince and Overton on 1st May 1649): "The people . . . shall chuse all their publicke Officers that are in any kinde to administer the Law for their respective places, for one whole year, and no longer, and so from yeer to yeer."

78 *Whisper*, p. 6; *Samaritane*, p. 64.

79 *Fountain*, p. 1.

80 A. O. Lovejoy rightly emphasises that Primitivism, contrary to some recent interpretations of it, nearly always implies "what may, in theological language, be called a Doctrine of the Fall": op. cit., Introduction, p. 17.

81 *Love*, pp. 3, 12–13. It is worth noting perhaps that Walwyn uses the word "natural" mainly in two senses: (1) sometimes as contrasted with "supernatural" (e.g. "very heathen and meere natural men," *Love*, p. 5); (2) more often as contrasted with "artificial" or "superfluous."

82 *Love*, p. 7.

83 *Fountain*, p. 22; *Vanitie*, p. 25.

84 *Love*, pp. 48–9.

85 *Samaritane*, pp. 33, 34.

86 *Vanitie*, p. 21.

87 *Love*, p. 44.

88 *Fountain*, pp. 25, 2.

89 Ibid., p. 22. For some of these points, cf. M. James, *Social Problems and Policy during the Puritan Revolution* (1930), and "The Political Importance of the Tithes Controversy . . . 1640–60," *History*, June 1941; E. Hughes, "The Development of Excise" (in *Studies in Administration and Finance* (1934)); C. Hill, "The Agrarian Legislation of the Interregnum," *English Historical Review*, April 1940.

90 Kiffin, *Wiles*, p. 15.

91 Ibid., p. 10.

92 *Fountain*, p. 18.

93 *Love*, pp. 2, 3.

94 Walwyn's "rationalism" was further distinguished from that of a later age

by his belief that "things divine . . . could never have beene perceived by the light of nature and reason" (*A Prediction of Mr. Edwards, His Conversion* (1646), p. 3), and that reason had to yield when it seemed to contradict the gospel (Brooke, *Charity*, p. 4).

⁹⁵ *Love*, p. 5.

⁹⁶ *Fountain*, pp. 1, 6.

⁹⁷ *Vanitie*, pp. 21, 42; *Love*, p. 7.

⁹⁸ *Petition* (1647), pp. 1, 4; cf. his share in the various Agreements of the People.

⁹⁹ *Love*, p. 41.

¹⁰⁰ *Samaritane*, p. 66.

¹⁰¹ E. Troeltsch, *The Social Teaching of the Christian Churches* (1931), i, 328–30 (cf. the present writer's article, "Ernst Troeltsch's Conception of History," *Dublin Review*, Jan. 1944).

¹⁰² *Petition* (1647), p. 5.

¹⁰³ *Physick*, pp. 4, 21, 29.

¹⁰⁴ Ibid., Advertisement. The identity of Walwyn the Leveller and Walwyn the Physician can be established in the following way: We know from Walwyn the Leveller's writings that he was born in Newland (Worcs.) in the year 1600 (*Fountain*, pp. 1, 2). The parish register of Newland notes the baptism of "William Walweyne the sonne of Robt Walwyne gent" on 17th August 1600 (I am indebted for this entry to Canon F. E. Hutchinson). Now in the family pedigree mentioned above, the entry for "William, son of Robert" runs thus: "William Walwyn of London, M.D., ob. circa 1680, mar. and had issue several dau's." (The M.D. is, I suggest, an excusable embellishment in the interests of family prestige.) The last will of Walwyn the Physician (now at Somerset House) is really dated 1680 and was proved on 14th January 1681 (New Style). Moreover, the picture in *Physick* (1681) bears the inscription: "Aetatis suae 80," which tallies with the date of his birth if we assume that it refers to the year of his death, immediately preceding the publication of *Physick for Families*.

CHAPTER FOUR

WERE THE LEVELLERS "LEVELLERS"?

To many anxious contemporaries, the Levellers seemed to aim at a complete social revolution marked by the "levelling" of rank and wealth. In Lilburne's case, as we have seen, this charge was quite unfounded; with regard to Walwyn, it was largely justified. It is, however, much more difficult to find out what their less articulate followers may have had in mind. Were they all mainly political radicals, staking their hopes on a wide extension of the franchise and the securing of certain fundamental rights, or were some of them trying to realise wider aims?

Lilburne tells us in a picturesque passage that many of his adherents were to be found among "the hobnails, clouted shoes, the private soldiers, the leather and woollen Aprons, and the laborious and industrious people in England."[1] The Leveller activities centred in London, but Leveller supporters can be traced in Surrey, Buckinghamshire, Hertfordshire, Oxfordshire, Devon, Cornwall, Pembrokeshire, Derbyshire, Lancashire, and as far north as Carlisle.[2] These were the men all over England among whom the Civil War had given rise to far-reaching hopes. Here is a typical example taken from a Leveller tract: "We received so many Promises, Declarations, and Remonstrances from the Parliament that . . . they would make us the absolute freest People in the world, removing all Oppressions; all which did engage us to assist them."[3] Later, the Army had revived these hopes by solemn promises to deliver the people "from all kinds of oppression, usurpation and Arbitrary Proceedings . . . that all the free-borne People of England might sit down in quiet under their own Vines under the glorious administration of Justice and Righteousnesse, and in full possession of [their] Fundamental Rights and Liberties."[4] The disillusionment was, therefore, all the greater on "finding both the Parliament and the Army to break their promises" and "to apostatize from their principles."[5] "Alas!" exclaimed a Hertfordshire Leveller in 1649, "the Countryman's heart is as full of grief, and his eyes as full of tears, as ever."[6] These men were more and more inclined to feel that they were not represented by any of the actors on the swiftly changing political scene; a Leveller pamphlet even contained the menacing question: "Is not all the controversie whose slaves the poor shall be?"[7]

The growth of this social discontent was probably fostered by the economic situation of the late 1640's. It is hazardous to generalise about the economic conditions of any period in the absence of reliable statistics, but it is known[8] that a succession of very bad harvests due to unfavourable weather ("summer and winter invading each other's quarters"[9]) resulted in exceptionally high wheat prices after 1646. The simultaneous complaints about the general decay of trading are too numerous to be entirely dismissed.[10] The Leveller agitation of the winter of 1647–8 was, at any rate, quite clearly bound up with the economic problems of the trading and working population of London. The Smithfield Petition (January 1648) implored Parliament to "consider that our estates are expended, the whole trade of the Nation decayed, thousands of families impoverished, and merciless Famine is entered into our Gates." Lilburne reinforced this point by telling a meeting of his friends what he had just heard from some Wiltshire clothiers: that those among them who had been able to give work to a hundred people could now employ only about a dozen, and that the poor in Wiltshire had forcibly taken away the peasants' corn as it was carried to the market.[11] The pamphlet supporting the Smithfield Petition was entitled: *The mournfull Cryes of many thousand poor Tradesmen, who are ready to famish through decay of Trade.* It used extremely strong language: "O heark, heark at our doors, how our children cry Bread, Bread, Bread; and we now, with bleeding hearts, cry once more to you, pity, pity an oppressed, inslaved

F

People: carry our cries . . . to the Parliament, and tell them, if
they be still deaf, the tears of the oppressed will wash away the
foundations of their houses." Parliament was blamed for the
economic crisis because of the "Taxes, Customs and Excize,
that compells the Country to raise the price of food, and to buy
nothing from us but meer absolute necessaries." Another cause
for complaint was found in the presence of the Army in London,
as a result of which, it was asserted, the value of English cur-
rency abroad was on the decline "and no Merchants beyond Sea
will trust their goods hither, and our own Merchants [will]
conveigh their Estates from hence,[12] . . . and then our Trade
will be utterly lost." It seems, in fact, that behind much of this
unrest was the fear of a second Civil War. "There are now
clouds of blood over our heads again," ran a letter from the
London Levellers to their friends in Kent, "and the very
rumours and fears of Warre hath . . . wasted Trading, and
enhaunsed the price of all food and cloathing. . . . Neither pen
nor tongue can express the misery, which will ensue immediately upon the beginning of another Warre."[13]

In these circumstances attacks on the privileged social classes
could be expected. "Mercurius Populi," a supporter of Lilburne
and the Army Levellers, spoke of clergymen, lawyers, nobility,
gentry and university men as "tyrants, oppressours and de-
ceivers," and explained the persistent failure of Parliament to
satisfy the grievances of the people by the fact that the members
of Parliament came from those classes.[14] The Hertfordshire
Levellers, drawing the same conclusion, announced their intention never "to chuse . . . for a Parliament man . . . lords of
Mannors, Im-propriators, and Lawyers, whose Interest is in
our oppression and at this day keep us in bondage like Egyptian
Task-masters."[15] (Such views must have added weight to the
Leveller demand for a new Parliament and to the reluctance, on
the part of the ruling groups, to grant it.) Kings, lords and
courtiers, according to "Mercurius Populi," were simply idle
men living on the fruit of the common people's labour.[16] The
London Levellers asked in a similar temper: "What are your
ruffling Silks and Velvets, and your glittering Gold and Silver

Laces? Are they not the sweat of our brows?"[17] The general conclusion was this: on the one side were all the oppressors who "buy large possessions in the earth and call their houses after their own names," and on the other side were the oppressed, "the lower sort of People" or "the meaner and poor People," "the laborious Husbandman, the Handicraftsman, and all kind of honest Tradesmen."[18] (It is interesting to note that the expression "the middle sort of men" could be used in the same sense; the difference between the middle class and their social inferiors was evidently not felt to be considerable, the dividing line ran above the "middle sort and poor People."[19]) The Hertfordshire Levellers even asserted that this division corresponded to the split between the two parties in the Civil War, which had been fought by men "whose interest was in the peoples oppression" against those who "were oppressed by great men."[20] It was something like a conspiracy of the rich, was another opinion, that made "a prey of the poor people."[21] These Levellers (we may think of them as representing the radical wing of the party) felt very strongly that there was a cleavage between the rich and the poor, between the "great men" and the "common people."

Like Lilburne, these men were convinced that England had been under a tyrannical régime ever since the Norman Conquest had brought to an end what they believed to have been something like a state of nature. In particular, they extolled the excellency of the Saxon legal practices abolished by William the Conqueror, and compared them angrily with the costly, inconvenient and dilatory proceedings of the "Norman law," made into an instrument of oppression by "the subtilty of the Lawyers."[22] Every man, was a typical demand, should "have Justice administered at his own doore, as in the dayes of King Edward and King Alfred."[23] "Strive to get your lawes made certain, short and plain" was another Leveller's advice to the people, "and your tryals in every hundred, as it was before the Norman Tyrant enslaved you."[24] The Buckinghamshire Levellers protested against "coming to Westminster" (which at that time was the seat of the law courts) and proclaimed that they would have nothing to do with lawyers, but would try to have all their controversies ended by two, three or twelve men of their neighbourhood, "as before the Norman Conquest."[25] The very language of the law was, of course, a reminder of its Norman origin. Translation into English and simplification were demanded again and again; the idea of a simple code of law in English, later to be taken up by the Barebone Parliament, occurs in a suggestion by an anonymous Leveller that all laws should be published in one book, a copy of which was to be kept in every parish church.[26]

The radical Levellers went further in their anti-Normanism than Lilburne, who confined his attacks to the "Norman" legal procedures; the "Norman" laws themselves came in for severe criticism. Most laws were unjust, stated a leading article in the Leveller paper, because they were "built by an unlawful, usurped and tyrannical power, . . . [the] Conqueror and his successors"; not even Magna Carta was excepted from this condemnation. Thus, it was concluded, "all the people of this Nation are yet slaves . . . being under the laws and government of William."[27] It must have seemed ominous to the new rulers of the Commonwealth that these words were written only a few months after the execution of a successor to William the Conqueror's throne. A little later the Hertfordshire Levellers also declared: "Government we see none, but the old tyrannical Norman Government."[28] The word "Norman" had evidently grown into a comprehensive term of abuse directed against all forms of "oppression" (something like Cobbett's "the Thing"). "Now is the most precious time, that hath been since the dayes of the conquest, for to shake off all . . . thraldome":[29] this kind of statement may appear vague, but if we take into account the keen resentment of social inequalities noticed above we may be able to understand why the Levellers aroused such anxiety in those unsettled and unsettling times.

The Buckinghamshire Levellers, justifying their social ideas, expressed their earnest belief that it was "the end of the redemption by Jesus, to restore all things"—and that restoration, they thought, implied equality, because before the Fall God had

allowed man to rule only over "inferior creatures, but not over
his own kinde." They left no doubt that they, unlike Lilburne,
were thinking particularly of economic equality: nobody, they
insisted, should be allowed "to enclose the creatures to his own
use, to the impoverishing of his neighbours."[30] It is clear that
their idea of equality was influenced by the passionate religious
inquiry around them. The scarcity and nature of the material at
our disposal do not, in many cases, allow us to discover how
far the other radical Levellers were connected with the spiritual
unrest of the time, but there is reason to believe that such a
connection existed. Ever since the early 1640's, when new
sects were springing up in such profusion and old ones were
rapidly gaining ground, it had been maintained by their opponents that they were spreading, not only religious heresy, but
social radicalism as well. At first, up to about 1646, this may
not have been the case. Not even the ever-watchful heresy-
hunter Thomas Edwards could, in the first part of his *Gangraena:
or a Catalogue of many of the Errours, Heresies, and pernitious
Practices of the Sectaries of this time* (February 1646), collect
more than a handful of socially dangerous beliefs among the
sectarians. True, "Anabaptists" were often alleged to be communists like their fanatical namesakes of Münster, but this was
never supported by any evidence at all. In the course of 1646,
however, the situation seems to have changed. In the later
parts of *Gangraena*, published in May and December of that
year, the references to political and social heresies were far
more frequent. In 1647 the authors of a joint declaration of
Independents and Baptists (among them W. Kiffin, Lilburne's
old friend) had to admit that "the erroneous opinions . . . of
some particular persons making profession of the same way,
and passing under the same denomination with the servants of
God themselves, have from time to time ministered occasion to
the ignorant and weak to misconceive . . . the state and temper
of the . . . people fearing God." From what follows it is clear
which errors were referred to: demands for social equality ("a
parity, or all to be equal in power") and communism ("a community amongst men in the good things of this life"). These

were repudiated at length, particularly the argument for communism based on the example of the Apostles (Acts ii, 44; iv, 35),[31] which is especially interesting because this very argument was used by Walwyn and also by the Buckinghamshire Levellers, who promised help to all "that joyn in community in Gods way, as those [in] Acts 2."[32]

There must have been, indeed, quite a number of Leveller supporters among the Baptist congregations. On two further occasions, in April and May 1649, Kiffin and other prominent Baptists found it necessary to dissociate themselves from the Levellers.[33] Lilburne and Overton, as we have seen, were Baptists, so were several active Army Levellers.[34] The very pamphlet that brought the Leveller leaders into the Tower was read in public meetings of the Baptists.[35] At the same critical time, in April and May 1649, the well-known Baptist minister, Edward Harrison, a Hertfordshire man, came forward in defence of the "Four worthy Asserters of Englands Liberties, now Prisoners in the Tower" and their "exquisite Model" of an Agreement, and Edward Barber, a Baptist merchant tailor of London, supported the Levellers' attempt "to take away all slaverie and tyrannie, brought in by Tyrants and their flatterers, in their Civill or Ecclesiasticall Government."[36] Among the Independents, too, there were some who had Leveller sympathies, especially in John Goodwin's church. That congregation spent fifty shillings towards the printing of one of Walwyn's pamphlets and supplied John Lilburne with the necessities of life while he was in prison.[37] In many cases, it is true, we cannot tell whether the sectarian Levellers belonged to the radical wing or not. We can only go so far as to say that, in view of the close connection between the Leveller movement as a whole and sectarian religion, the radical Levellers probably did not escape this influence, and that some sectarians showed "levelling" tendencies.

In common with the general tendency among the sectarians, the anticlericalism of the Leveller rank and file was very marked. "Why," asked "Mercurius Populi," "are Clergymen still so high in your esteem? Seeing . . . they bring you only

their own various and doubtfull opinions?"[38] The *Moderate*
was echoing a current opinion when it spoke of ministers as
called "by Oxford and Cambridge, but whether by Christ is
questionable";[39] this view was, for example, powerfully spread
by John Saltmarsh, an Army chaplain and himself a supporter of
the Army Levellers.[40] To "Mercurius Populi," the universities
were "dennes of Foxes and nests of Vipers"; ministers were no
more "priests than the common people, who were reasonable
creatures, in possession of God's word and therefore not in need
of any clerical help."[41]

Such anticlericalism was, of course, the religious basis for the
Levellers' strong stand against the compulsory payment of
tithes—an ever-recurring item in their tracts. M. James has
shown that the tithes controversy in the Puritan Revolution was
fraught with radical possibilities, especially as many tithes,
owing to the spoliation of ecclesiastical property during the
sixteenth century, were now in the hands of lay owners, the
so-called impropriators. There was some justification for the
fear expressed by some members of Parliament that "tenants
who were asking to be quit of tithes would soon ask to be quit
of rent."[42] Hertfordshire, a stronghold of the radical Levellers,
produced a remarkable anti-tithe petition containing a reference
to the "griping landlords" and the complaint that "the husbandman's labour is envied him; and others . . . live upon his
labour." Similarly, the Hertfordshire Levellers referred to both
lords of manors and impropriators as "Gyants of Self-interest"
and attacked injustices of both copyholds and tithes.[43] One
Leveller group was even prepared to support the agrarian communism of the Diggers, and the author of some leading articles
in the *Moderate* was probably influenced by Digger ideas when
he called private property "the ground of all Civil Offences"
and "the greatest cause of most sins against the Heavenly
Deity."[44]

Communist views, however, are extremely rare in Leveller
writings.[45] Nor is there any reason to believe that all Levellers
had a share in such social radicalism as we can trace among them.
To restore the balance we should remind ourselves that there

seems to have been widespread support for the fairly moderate Leveller petitions and Lilburne's Agreement of the People. Many of Lilburne's followers were probably quite content with his political programme pure and simple. This seems to have been the case especially among the Army Levellers. None of the Leveller spokesmen in the Putney debates pressed for more than political equality as expressed in Rainborough's famous statement: "Really I think that the poorest he that is in England hath a life to live, as the greatest he; and therefore truly, sir, I think it's clear, that every man that is to live under a government ought first by his own consent to put himself under that government."[46] Even Sexby, the unruliest of the Agitators, did not show any intention of going beyond the Agreement of the People. The same is true of most of the petitions presented by the soldiers of certain regiments. Only now and again such documents included demands for the abolition of tithes, legal reforms, the restoration of enclosed common land, or the relief of the poor,[47] but they very often insisted on provisions which were of interest only to soldiers: higher rates of pay, payment of arrears, indemnity for acts of war, support for widows and orphans, etc. Like all armies, the New Model was somewhat divorced from civilian life and therefore not so susceptible to civilian needs.

Once again, however, attention should be paid to the religious situation. One should bear in mind the special hopes and expectations nourished by the peculiar spiritual atmosphere of the New Model. The conventional picture of the Puritan soldier with the Bible in his knapsack may not correspond to reality,[48] but it is a fact that at least a vocal minority believed themselves to be fighting for God's cause. Some of them went further still by proclaiming that God would, through them, establish His kingdom on earth. Men like Colonel Thomas Harrison and Lieutenant-Colonel William Goffe were deeply convinced of this, and there were moments when they found a willing listener in Oliver Cromwell. These soldiers anticipated a spiritual mood current among sectarians outside the Army a few years later; the origin of the Fifth Monarchy Men can, indeed, be

traced to these Army circles. We shall see later how much
social radicalism was linked with the various millenarian ideas
of the 1650's, and this may well have been the case earlier as
well. The millenarian Thomas Collier, for example, in a sermon
preached during the Putney debates on the text, "Behold I
create new heavens and a new earth," put forward many of the
Leveller demands (especially law reform and the abolition of
tithes) and exhorted the army "to undo every yoke" and to
remove "whatsoever bears but the face of oppression in it."[49]
Thus, radical tendencies elsewhere allied with the Leveller
movement might in the army have come under the influence of
millenarian hopes. As all students of Puritanism know, it is
impossible to draw hard and fast dividing lines between the
various Puritan groups. There were, in fact, some members of
the army who combined a belief in the Second Coming of
Christ with Leveller sympathies. Major Francis White, a friend
of the Agitators, wrote in 1649: "Now are those last and great
commotions begun which our Saviour Christ fore-told, wherein
should be warres and rumours of warres before the time of his
coming to raigne as King upon his holy hill of Zion."[50]
Lieutenant-Colonel John Jubbes, the author of an Agreement of
the People closely modelled on that of the Levellers, was confi-
dently looking forward to the personal reign of Christ on earth.[51]
Captain William Bray, who was imprisoned after the first
Leveller mutiny in November 1647 and expelled from the army
in March 1649 when fresh mutinies were in the air, proclaimed
during his imprisonment: "I see a power of a more glorious
constitution [than the present one] . . . This doth appear but
as a Starre, but where this true Starre appears, the Sun is turned
into darknesse and the Moon into bloud. . . . The day of the
Lord is comming upon the Lords earth, and upon the Lords and
Commons of the earth."[52] John Saltmarsh, the inspiring chaplain, should also be mentioned here: he was, as we shall see,
both the prophet of a spiritual millennium and a supporter of the
Leveller mutineers of 1647. It remains uncertain what these
men expected the millennium to bring, but they evidently did
not regard the Leveller programme as an end in itself and may

have had radical hopes for the establishment of social justice. They may well have agreed with some of Lilburne's enthusiastic followers who predicted that God would "establish his Throne on earth . . . by which means the destroyer shall be destroyed, and the oppressor oppressed; then shall his captives go free, and his prisoners be set at liberty."[53]

So far we have had to gather our evidence for this chapter mainly from collective pronouncements or from the occasional writings of obscure individuals; in such cases it is not always possible to penetrate very far into the minds of the authors. There is, fortunately, one member of the Leveller rank and file of whom a fuller portrait can be attempted: Samuel Chidley, by trade a well-to-do seller of stockings in London.[54] His mother, Katherine, a member of an Independent congregation, must have been something of an original. She was one of the first women to claim and exercise the right of preaching in church and engaged in a spirited pamphlet war with Thomas Edwards, who was duly shocked by these first-fruits of female emancipation and called her a "brasen-faced audacious old woman."[55] Her son was, as one might have expected, a dyed-in-the-wool sectarian. "God's people," he wrote, "have been from the beginning and ought to be an holy, speciall, and peculiar people separated from sinners . . . in spirituall worship"; "heaven must be begun by a separation from the children of darkness upon earth."[56] Early on he became acquainted with John Lilburne; he knew him "from the time of his sufferings by the bloody Bishops"[57] and remained faithful to him ever after. Attempting, together with Lilburne, to witness "against the corrupt and abused authorities" in temporal as well as spiritual matters, he was not able to avoid spending some time in prison. In November 1647 he was committed to the Gatehouse for supporting the first Leveller petition after it had been voted seditious by the House of Commons and burned by the hangman.[58] He was back among the Levellers when the Smithfield Petition was being discussed early in 1648; on that occasion he was appointed one of the treasurers of the party.[59] Later he served as an official of the Register for Debentures (the certificates which were given to soldiers pending the payment of their arrears) and this work brought him into close contact with soldiers and ex-soldiers. It was in this way that he "was more acquainted with the sorrows and grievances of the Nation than before" and saw more clearly how the "selfish cares of the world choaked . . . the men of high degree";[60] perhaps he meant to imply by this statement that he now regarded the earlier Leveller programme as inadequate. In an attractive passage he explained why he felt it necessary to intervene on behalf of the soldiers: "Were it not to satisfie an afflicted, poor, distressed, and needy People, who are almost spent for want of pure Justice . . . I should not be so forward to write, and print Books . . . but rather sit and see at distance, and hold my peace till I have learned wisdom, esteeming it better to live in quietnes, and remain private in the watch tower of observation, to take an exact view of all things."[61] We now know that he was not exaggerating the seriousness of the soldiers' grievance when he wrote: "Many could not have satisfaction for their Arreares . . . unless they would sell the same at an inconsiderable value, or double the like sums upon the Credit of the Common-wealth, which abundance of them could not do. . . . Many have been forced through their extream necessity to sell their Bills and Debts for 5s., 4s., 3s., yea, less than 2s. per pound."[62] Chidley was much too interested in altering this state of affairs to remain in office for long. Even after his dismissal (in 1651 or 1652) he kept on pressing the case of the debenture-holders by constant petitions to Parliament—without any avail.

There is a letter extant which Chidley wrote to Oliver Cromwell in February 1651. (His acquaintance with Cromwell was of long standing: he had met him at the beginning of the Long Parliament and had conferred with him on social questions in 1649.) In this letter, in addition to reminding Cromwell of the soldiers' arrears, he developed his programme of social reform. He suggested that committees for the hearing of complaints and the redressing of grievances should be set up in every county and city, consisting "rather of approved faithfull men than of great men," and that these committees should be changed every year. No lawsuit should be allowed to take longer than one year. Tithes should be abolished ("the clergie should learne to work with their hands, as both Paul and many better men then they did"), and excise, which fell heavily on the shoulders of the poor, should be replaced by a subsidy to be collected from the rich. In this way, he thought, "justice, tranquilitie, peace and prosperitie would be advanced" and the "wofull cryes of the poore" would cease.[63]

It was characteristic of this man (the prototype of many Puritan reformers after his day) that he was capable of undertaking a one-man crusade to bring about a reform which he felt to be particularly urgent. To him, as to a number of his contemporaries,[64] it appeared monstrous that people should be put to death for theft, especially as their crime may have been caused by sheer poverty. In order to get this law changed he petitioned the Lord Mayor of London; addressed the Commissioners of Oyer and Terminer at Newgate; wrote a pamphlet called *A Cry against a Crying Sinne* and had it printed in red letters; forced the pamphlet on Lord President Bradshaw and begged him to read it to the Council of State; drew the attention of Parliament to it; and finally, on the next execution for theft at Tyburn, "elbowed his way through the crowd, nailed his pamphlet on a tree that stood by the gallows and wrote this warning above:

> Cursed be that bloody hand
> Which takes this down without command."[65]

There can be no doubt about the spiritual source of this energy. To Chidley, no law of any authority was valid unless it agreed with "the Law of him who is higher than the Highest"; in working for a just cause he felt to have "a designe . . . for God."[66] True, he did not escape some characteristically Puritan prejudices. He could, for example, wax exceedingly indignant about "Popish" bells (those "abominable Idols") and cathedral churches ("those old Chyming chimneys of the druncken whore of Babylon").[67] Along with such dislikes, however, his intense reading of the Scriptures had revealed to him "the oppressions that are done under the sun" and enabled him to judge the great ones of this world with remarkable independence. The resulting state of his mind is most impressively shown in one of his pamphlets which contains an allegory on Old Testament motives (a "fantasy" almost, in the musical sense of the word), meant as a warning for Cromwell. In view of his relations with Cromwell he may have been entitled to expect that these words would come to the great man's notice. This passage reads:

> The entertainment which I shal give him [i.e. Cromwell] in these sad and unsetled times is to lead him by the waters of Marah, in the valey of weeping to the house of mourning, the storehouse for tears, where the hearts of the wise frequently retire, and the Widdows by the sides of the house are set like weeping Vines, and the Fatherless children like the plants thereof, round about the tables of contempt, feeding on the bread of sorrows, and drinking tears in an abundant measure. . . . Not far from this Mansion house, there is a place where is the throne of Judgment, with six steps. At the end of the said steps are twelve Lyons, six on the one side, and six on the other, answerable to the 12 Princes of the Tribes of Israel, or the Lambs twelve Apostles: And there is no other Jury. Priviledge of Parliament cannot here be pleaded, there being a prerogative power above it.
> The Statutes of Omri[68] are all here condemned to be burnt in great contempt.
> And a Law established which will serve all Nations.
> This is a Court of Justice and Equity too, where whores and harlots, and all others may have free liberty to plead their causes without seeing a Lawyer.[69]

There is more in this than genuine emotion. The writer's words, moulded by the powerful images of prophetic religion and grounded on firm standards of social justice, acquired an impersonal, objective force. Only thus could a stocking-seller from London (and, we may add, a tinker from Bedford) write with such simple grandeur.

What then of our initial question? To what extent were the Levellers "levellers"? A complete answer cannot be given.

Some undoubtedly were, others were not, and it is impossible to determine the proportionate strength of those tendencies. This, after all, would be far from easy even in the case of a political party of our own time, in spite of "mass observation" and "Gallup polls." A well-informed contemporary observer believed that the "levelling" wing was in the minority. "A pestilence," he addressed the Levellers, ". . . hath been knowne to have infected some that frequent your meetings. . . . 'Tis the doctrine of Parity or levelling, bringing all mens Estates to an Equallity. . . . And however the Croud of those that follow you intend no such thing . . . yet just suspition is upon many of you."[70] This may well have been the case. We can, at any rate, confirm the opinion of a Leveller renegade who wrote: "We were an Heterogenial Body, consisting of parts very diverse from another, setled upon principles inconsistent one with another."[71]

Because of these divergencies any statements about the Levellers as a whole must be treated with great care. Such statements are generally based on Lilburne's writings, but although the vocal Lilburne had many followers, the quieter Walwyn may have had his quiet adherents. Nor is it safe to build too much on the "official" Leveller declarations which, like all similar documents, were arrived at by compromise and destined for a particular political situation. A democratic posterity naturally attaches most importance to the Levellers' democratic proposals, but to some of the Levellers themselves this does not seem to have been the predominant issue. Enough has been said above to suggest that, in some cases, the elusive spirit behind the words and actions was actually or potentially more radical than the Agreement of the People. Demands for legal reform or the abolition of tithes, not in themselves revolutionary, could easily become more threatening if they were accompanied by that bitter awareness of a social cleavage which we have noticed above, or by searching social criticism such as Walwyn's. Nor was it possible to predict the consequences of Chidley's burning zeal for social justice. The radical Levellers, inspired by beliefs derived from both books of the Scriptures and by various conceptions of a state of nature, envisaged a federation of small communities of neighbours, fairly equal in ownership and status, ruling themselves without the interference of professional magistrates or lawyers according to simple and well-known laws. This ideal, as we have seen, was not entirely absent from Lilburne's mind, but in his case it was obscured by his preoccupation with purely political reforms and the limitations of his desire for equality. Lilburne's chief aim, we might sum up, was equality before the law; that of his more radical friends, equality established by law.

NOTES TO CHAPTER FOUR

[1] Lilburne, *The Upright Mans Vindication* (1653), p. 15.

[2] Cf. especially the Leveller weekly news-sheet, *Moderate*, July 1648–Sept. 1649.

[3] *Declaration of the Wel-Affected in the County of Buckinghamshire* [10th May 1649], p. 4. (The date in [ ] is the one under which an anonymous tract can be found in the Catalogue of the Thomason Collection.) This pamphlet has sometimes been regarded as a Digger production, but Petegorsky has shown that it was the pronouncement of a Leveller group (Petegorsky, *Left-Wing Democracy in the English Civil War*, p. 138).

[4] *Petition* [1st Sept. 1650], p. 1. (Cf. *A Representation of the Army*, 14th June 1647; Woodhouse, *Puritanism and Liberty*, p. 403.)

[5] *Declaration* (Bucks.), p. 4.

[6] Edward Harrison, *Plain Dealing or the Countrymans doleful Complaint* (1649), p. 11.

[7] *The mournfull Cryes of many thousand poor Tradesmen*, printed in Anon., *Declaration of some Proceedings of Lt.-Col. John Lilburne* (1648).

[8] Thorold Rogers, *History of Agriculture and Prices*, v, 203–7, 826.

[9] W. Sedgwick, *The Leaves of the Trees of Life* (1648), p. 24.

[10] Cf., e.g., *Two knaves for a penny* [28th Oct.] 1647, p. 8; R. L., *Free Mans Plea for Freedom* [18th May] 1648, p. 12; *Moderate Intelligencer*, 22nd–29th March 1649; *Moderate*, 17–24th April, 24th April–1st May, 15th–22nd May, 29th May–5th June, 14th–21st Aug. 1649. (See also M. James, *Social Problems*, passim.)

[11] Lilburne, *An Impeachment of High Treason Against Oliver Cromwell* (1649), p. 37. Cf. G. D. Ramsay, *The Wiltshire Woollen Industry in the 16th and 17th centuries* (1943), p. 112.

[12] A marginal note emphasised that the flight of capital had already begun: "The Merchants have already kept back from the Tower many hundred thousand pounds, and no bullion is brought into the Tower, so that mony will be more scarce daily."

[13] *A Declaration of Some Proceedings of Lt.-Col. John Lilburn* (1648), pp. 27, 53–4, 55–6.

14 *Mercurius Populi* [11th Nov. 1647], pp. 3, 4.

15 *A Declaration of divers of the Inhabitants of the County of Hartford.* [4th Feb. 1650], p. 7. ("Impropriators" are lay owners of tithes.)

16 *Mercurius Populi*, p. 4.

17 *Declaration of some Proceedings of Lt.-Col. John Lilburne*, p. 52.

18 *Moderate*, 3rd–10th July 1649; *Declaration* (Bucks.), pp. 3, 4; *Proposals in behalfe of the Poor of this Nation* [2nd Aug. 1653], p. 4. (The last-named tract is not a Leveller publication.)

19 *Declaration* (Bucks.), title-page, p. 3. Cf. Tawney, *The Agrarian Problem in the Sixteenth Century*, pp. 207–8.

20 *Declaration* (Herts.), p. 4.

21 *Moderate* 13–20th March 1649, Letter from Tewkesbury, 17th March.

22 *Declaration* (Herts.), p. 4.

23 James Frese, *Why not* (1649). (Frese was a free-lance supporter of the Leveller programme.)

24 *Mercurius Populi*, p. 5.

25 *Declaration* (Bucks.), p. 7.

26 *The Representative of Divers well-affected persons in and about the City of London.* . . . [6th Feb. 1649], pp. 13–14.

27 *Moderate*, 3rd–10th April 1649; 31st Oct.–7th Nov. 1649.

28 *Declaration* (Herts.), p. 6. Cf. *Declaration* (Bucks.), p. 7: "We protest against the whole Norman power," followed by a very varied list of grievances.

29 *Mercurius Populi*, p. 5.

30 *Light Shining in Buckinghamshire* [5th Dec. 1648], pp. 5, 1, 2.

31 *A Declaration by Congregationall Societies in and about the City of London, as well of those commonly called Anabaptists, as others* [22nd Nov.] 1647. (Printed in *Confessions of Faith*, Hansard Knollys Society, 1854, p. 273 seq.)

32 *Declaration* (Bucks.), p. 7.

33 W. Kiffin, and others, *The humble Petition and Representation of the several Churches of God in London, commonly (though falsly) called Anabaptists* (April 1649); *Walwins Wiles* (May 1649).

34 L. F. Brown, *The Political Activities of the Baptists and Fifth Monarchy Men* (1912), p. 10.

35 Lilburne, *The Picture of the Councel of State* (1649), p. 42.

36 Edward Harrison, *Plain Dealing* (May 1649), p. 16; Edward Barber, *An Answer to the Essex Watchmans Watchword* (April 1649), p. 8.

37 Pease, *The Leveller Movement*, p. 251; Lilburne, *Jonahs Cry* (1647), p. 5.

38 *Mercurius Populi*, p. 4.

39 *Moderate*, 22nd–29th Aug. 1648.

40 William Dell, who held similar views, was known to the Hertfordshire Levellers: *Declaration* (Herts.), p. 2.

41 *Mercurius Populi*, pp. 4, 2.

42 M. James, "The Political Importance of the Tithes Controversy in the English Revolution, 1640–60," *History*, June 1941, p. 9.

43 W. Urwick, *Nonconformity in Hertfordshire* (1884), pp. 832, 141; *Declaration* (Herts.), pp. 5, 4.

44 *Moderate*, 31st July–7th Aug., 4–11th Sept. 1649. The question of the leading articles in the *Moderate* deserves brief consideration. They contain comments on political and religious matters, and some of them are of a fairly high quality. At least two different writers can be distinguished; the author of the leading articles after 9th February 1649 was far more concerned with social questions and altogether more radical. Haller and Davies (*Leveller Tracts 1647–1653*, p. 20) assume the editorship of Gilbert Mabbot, one of the official licensers of the

press, whose imprimatur regularly appears on this news-sheet. A denial of Mabbot's editorship appeared in the *Moderate* of 26th Sept.–3rd Oct. 1648. It seems that our evidence does not suffice to identify the editor (or editors).

45 I have found only those quoted in this chapter and in Chapter Three.

46 Woodhouse, *Puritanism and Liberty*, p. 53.

47 *The Case of the Army Truly Stated* (1647); Woodhouse, op. cit., p. 436; *Moderate*, 20–27th Feb. 1649; 21st–28th Nov. 1648; 18–25th Sept. 1649; *The Humble Representation of the Desires of the Officers and Souldiers in the Regiment of Horse for the County of Northumberland* [5th Dec. 1648]. War service has prevented me from consulting the Clarke MSS. at Worcester College, Oxford; they may contain some additional evidence on this point.

48 G. Davies, whose knowledge of Cromwell's army is unrivalled among living historians, has recently expressed his doubts about the extent of the New Model's religious enthusiasm: *Huntington Library Quarterly*, iv, 2, 180.

49 Woodhouse, op. cit., p. 395.

50 F. White, *A True Relation of the Proceedings in the Businesse of Burford* (1649), p. 15.

51 Jubbes, *Apology* (1649), p. 18 (cf. Appendix B).

52 W. Bray, *A Representation to the Nation . . . and more especially to those that are sanctified in God the Father according to Jesus Christ* (1648).

53 *A Letter from the North* [19th Sept. 1653], Preface.

54 He may have had connections with Hertfordshire: in 1650 he purchased Hitchin Manor. (R. L. Hine, *History of Hitchin* (1927), i, 212. This book contains a slight biographical sketch of Chidley.)

55 T. Edwards, *The third Part of Gangraena* (1646), p. 171.

56 S. Chidley, *An Additional Remonstrance to the Valiant and well-deserving Souldier, and the rest of the Creditors of the Common-wealth* (1653), p. 13; *Original Letters . . . Addressed to Oliver Cromwell . . .*, ed. by John Nickalls (1743), p. 59.

57 S. Chidley, *The Dissembling Scot Set forth in his Coulours or a Vindication of Lieu-Col. John Lilburn* (1652), p. 4.

58 Commons' Journals, 10th Nov. 1647.

59 *Declaration of Some Proceedings of Lt.-Col. John Lilburn* (1648), p. 17.

60 S. Chidley, *A Remonstrance To the valiant and well-deserving Souldiers and the rest of the Creditors of the Common-Wealth* (1653), pp. 16, 9.

61 Chidley, *Additional Remonstrance*, p. 4.

62 Chidley, *Remonstrance*, pp. 5, 6. For other evidence on this subject (especially the practice of doubling), cf. C. Hill, "The Agrarian Legislation of the Interregnum," *English Historical Review*, April 1940.

63 *Original Letters to Cromwell*, pp. 59, 60 (cf. note 56 above).

64 An Army Leveller, Nicholas Cowling, was also concerned about this: "Let the lives of men and women be no more trifled away at the pleasure of merciless Judges for inconsiderable values" (*A Survey of Tyrannie* (1650), p. 37).

65 R. L. Hine, op. cit., i, 213–15.

66 Chidley, *A Cry against a Crying Sinne* (1652), p. 3; *Remonstrance*, p. 14.

67 Chidley, *Bells Founder Confounded* [no date], p. 2; *Thunder from the Throne of God against the Temples of Idols* (1653), p. 1.

68 A King of Israel: 1 Kings xvi, 16.

69 Chidley, *Additional Remonstrance*, p. 12.

70 *Declaration of some Proceedings of Lt.-Col. John Lilburn*, p. 57.

71 Henry Denne, *The Levellers Designe Discovered* (1649), p. 8.

CHAPTER FIVE

THE RELIGION OF THE SPIRIT

I

THE discontinuation, in September 1649, of the Leveller news-sheet, the *Moderate*, marked the end of the Leveller movement. In that month the last Leveller mutiny in the army was suppressed. The rest of the Army Levellers must have conformed, some of them perhaps for a price in the shape of Irish lands. Lilburne still retained his personal popularity with the Londoners, but he was now merely pleading individual causes of other men or his own. Overton and Sexby went in for spying and conspiracy, Wildman divided his time between debates, intrigues and extensive land-speculation, Walwyn, we may assume, withdrew to his library, and Chidley tried to carry on in his own way. The social discontent of the 1650's was mainly represented by other men (though among them, as we shall see, some of the Leveller ideas continued to be alive). Most of these new radicals were connected with a further religious development among the Puritan sectarians which began in the late 1640's and gathered strength throughout the 1650's. Much of that urge towards a renewed inwardness was bound up with a certain conception of the "Spirit," and it is to this word that we must devote some attention if we wish to understand it.

In order to do so we must, for a while, leave the busy streets and the excited conventicles of London, and enter the quiet seclusion of Eton and Cambridge. Eton was the home of the "ever-memorable" *John Hales* (1584–1656),[1] a Fellow of that College since 1613. As a young man he had helped Sir Henry Savile to prepare the celebrated edition of St. Chrysostom's works, and the Fathers of the Church remained the object of his

82

Vera effigies doctiſſimi Viri
D. JOHANNIS HALES Colleg.Eton.Socij
et Eccles.Colleg.Windeſorienſis Canonici.

JOHN HALES

from Golden Remains of the Ever-Memorable
Mr. John Hales, 1659   (*British Museum*)

special interest throughout his life. He did not publish much during his lifetime, but his numerous friends, often coming to him for advice and instruction, were full of praise for the particularly clear and comprehensive mind and the immense but lightly borne learning of this kindly and modest man. Looking out on the world of the Thirty Years' War, Hales was immensely grieved to see that the religion of love gave rise to so much hatred; "nothing troubled him more," wrote Clarendon, "than the brawls which were grown from religion." To him the theological controversies of his time seemed to be about "conceits" and "opinions," not about religion at all. Like his friend Chillingworth, the author of the famous *Religion of Protestants*, he believed that there could be no doubt whatever about the fundamentals of Christianity. If we concentrated on the essentials, "we might in hearts be united, though in our tongues we were divided." It is "the unity of the Spirit in the bond of peace" (Eph. iv, 3), and not identity of conceit, which the Holy Ghost requires at the hands of Christians.[2]

It was, then, the spirit of the one Christian religion that mattered, not the letter of one of its sects. Hales was, however, aware that many ambiguities and dangers were concealed by the term "spirit." He taught that there were two meanings of this word: it could either mean "a secret elapse of supernatural influence of God upon the hearts of men, by which he is supposed inwardly to incline, inform and direct men in their ways and wills," or else it could indicate that part of our nature "which is opposed against the flesh, and which denominates us spiritual men." To avoid all misunderstandings Hales declared firmly: "The Spirit in the second sense is that I contend for; and this is nothing but reason illuminated by revelation out of the written word."[3]

Not only was human reason, guided by divine revelation— *recta ratio*—sufficient to lead men to salvation, but this powerful help was offered to all men without exception, and it was certainly not necessary to have any special learning for this purpose; Scripture, wrote Chillingworth, was "sufficiently intelligible to all that have understanding, whether they be learned or unlearned. . . . Nothing is necessary to be believed but what is plainly revealed."[4] There were some, it is true, who did not make proper use of their opportunity; we were bound to believe that in the end there would be "a select and chosen company of God." But it was not up to us to determine who would belong to it; meanwhile it was a precept of charity to presume a spiritual equality and to suppose that everyone professing the name of Christ was "of his fold."[5]

All these ideas were fully shared by the leading thinkers of the *Cambridge School of Platonism*—Benjamin Whichcote (1610–83), John Smith (1618–52), Ralph Cudworth (1617–88), and Henry More (1614–87). They too were opposed to the "captious niceties" and "deep speculation" of school theology, for "the way to heaven is plain and easy, if we have but honest hearts."[6] The soul of man was kindled from within by the spirit which was, as Whichcote put it, anticipating the famous Quaker expression, "the candle of the Lord lighted by God, and lighting man to God."[7] Unless the soul was kindled, all religion was empty talk, "a Doctrine that is wrapt up in Ink and Paper."[8] "As the eye cannot behold the sun," wrote John Smith, following Plotinus, "unless it be sunlike . . ., so neither can the soul of man behold God . . ., unless it be God-like, hath God formed in it, and be made partaker of the Divine Nature."[9]

Man could therefore know of God only because he had been created in the image of God and there was, in spite of his Fall, something of God in him. Now God was a rational being Himself and had illuminated man with "right reason." Any attempt to depreciate reason in the name of religion would therefore mean "to go against God," because reason was "the very voice of God."[10] There were, of course, supernatural truths which unaided reason was unable to discover; they were higher than human reason, but not opposed to it. Reason and faith were mutually dependent parts of the same structure, and not, as in the Puritan scheme of nature and grace, separated by an unbridgeable gulf. These Christian humanists were then, once again, attempting a synthesis of reason and faith; their main concern, just as that of many others before and after them, was to preserve the precarious balance between classical philosophy and the religion of Christ.

II

When Whichcote and Henry More were undergraduates at Cambridge they had a gifted contemporary in *John Saltmarsh*, who took his M.A. in 1636 at Magdalene College and was soon to become an influential teacher of the "Religion of the Spirit."[11] Before leaving the university this young divine published a slim volume of religious poems in Latin and English,[12] which revealed his preoccupation with the metaphysical thought and poetry of the day. One of these poems, called "A Meditation upon Eternitie," may be quoted here both for its intrinsic merit and the glimpse it affords of the author's mind.

> Methought I had a Clepsydra so wide,
> It held the ocean in his proudest tide:
> I still'd by teares, by drops, this watrie main;
> Yet I was glad to fill my glasse again.

> Then all the sands, all atomes of the aire
> I did imprison in a glasse: with care
> I let the dusty minutes single passe
> To the last atome; yet I turn'd the glasse.

> Methought I had a clock hung at a starre:
> My fancie spun the lines, the plummets were
> Ty'd too, which reacht the centre that low stop;
> Yet these runne down: again I wound them up.

> Then when I saw Eternitie outgo
> My clock, my glasse scorn'd to be measur'd so;
> I spy'd an Angel hover, and did crie
> To him, What's this you style Eternitie?

> He spoke thus in his momentanie stay,
> Go pluck from time his winged Yesterday
> And his Tomorrow. Then I askt him, How
> Call you it? So he answer'd me, A now.

> Then shew'd a circle uniform and round,
> And pointed to a chair set on the ground.
> I weary with enquiries, thought me blest,
> Sat in this embleme of eternall rest.

This, though hardly original, shows considerable talent; the last stanza in particular is truly akin to, not a mere imitation of, George Herbert's work. No further poetry, however, was to come from this thoughtful young man. Instead, he began to write religious prose of a high quality, rich in thought and imagery. From 1640 onwards, it must be added, he came under the spell of the Puritan sectarians and soon took an active part in the development of their ideas.

Like Hales and the Cambridge Platonists, Saltmarsh was appalled by the violent religious struggles of his time and sought to overcome the divisions by a renewal of the true spirit of Christianity. "Consider," he wrote, "that we may be one in one Christ though we think diversely."[13] To him, the true Church was an invisible community of those who were "baptised by one Spirit into oneness and unity"; any reliance on outward forms of church government was "but a finer kind of idolatry," often leading to its coarser kind and ending in the persecution of fellow Christians. He too thought that salvation was "plain, easy, and simply revealed," and that the Spirit could be heard in all men, the highest as well as the meanest. It was indeed, he believed, Christ Himself who was prepared to dwell in each one of us, perpetually giving and renewing life.[14]

Was this simply another way of referring to the Platonists' "candle of the Lord"? Here it would be best to remind ourselves of Hales' distinction between the two meanings of the word "spirit." Can Saltmarsh's fundamental idea be described, in Hales' words, as "reason illuminated by revelation"? The answer cannot be in doubt: Saltmarsh despised human reason and rejected humanism. "[I dare not] take my discoveries of Christ from Reason," he declared, "nor seek the glory of Him in Forms so much below Him."[15] It was, he thought, characteristic of the Christian religion that, unlike all other religions, it was not "founded upon reason and nature."[16] He insisted, therefore, that one should free oneself from "vaine Philosophie" and "the wisdom of the Greek."[17]

We thus arrive at the melancholy conclusion that the very idea on which all these men based their hopes for peace among

Christians could be the source of new divisions. The Puritan Saltmarsh, contrary to Hales and the Platonists, had come to accept the discrepancy between reason and faith. Human reason, in this view, was of no help at all in religious matters. By disregarding it something infinitely valuable could be gained: direct communion with God. The peculiar atmosphere of Puritan religious life, it is well known, was favourable to the growth of prophetic religion. At their conversion and often on subsequent occasions, many Puritans of all shades experienced "supernatural influences" of the Spirit, and these "breathings of God" sometimes forced them to proclaim their message to all the world.

It was in this way that Saltmarsh, instead of using his gifts only as a scholar or divine, became a prophet of the Lord. From his spiritual theology he came to derive the belief in a future Age of the Spirit. This idea belonged to a theological scheme of history going as far back as Joachim of Flora, the Calabrese monk of the twelfth century (in Dante's *Paradiso* described as "di spirito profetico dotato"). According to this powerful teaching, there were three ages of the world and three corresponding revelations: the Age of Law with the Old Testament revealing the Father; the Age of Grace with the New Testament revealing the Son; and the Age of the Spirit with the *Evangelium Aeternum*, a revelation yet to come.[18] The ground for the acceptance of such ideas in the 1640's had undoubtedly been prepared by Antinomianism, but this further step implied something of decisive importance: the conviction that the New Testament was not the last Word of God. It is well to remember that the development within Puritanism itself could easily be fitted into this scheme. The theology of the earlier Puritans had been greatly influenced by their awe-inspiring conception of God the Lawgiver and Judge, derived from the Old Testament. Next had come the Antinomian phase during which Christ and the Grace flowing from His Gospel had dominated religious thought. Now it was the turn of a theology centring round the Third Person of the Trinity.

In the course of the Civil War, in 1645 or 1646, Saltmarsh

seems to have arrived at the conclusion that the time of the last revelation was drawing nigh. "The warres in the severall States of Christendome," he wrote, "as Germany, Denmark, Italy, Ireland, England, etc. . . . . fall in their severall degrees and orders into the designe of God for his Church, and the ruine of Antichrist." Other indications of the impending event were: "The means of grace poured out so effectually in Preaching, and prophesying, and prayer amongst us. . . . The Gospel lightning from many Treatises, Discourses, Expositions. . . . The spring-ing up of many young Prophets. . . . To these, the meltings and dissolvings of customes, traditions, superstitions." The old order, he thought, would come to an end in not much more than six years.[19] In 1646 he became a chaplain in the New Model, probably in the belief that it was the instrument chosen by God for His great change.

In the army he and the like-minded William Dell were, to Richard Baxter's dismay, "the two great Preachers at the Head Quarters."[20] In June or July 1647 Saltmarsh wrote: "There is a mighty spirit raised up in the Army for Justice and Righteous-nesse; we admire at it."[21] This statement reflected the unity which pervaded in the army at that time, but a premonition where his sympathies would lie in the future was contained in his reference to the country being "much troubled about the burning of some Petitions"[22]—the Leveller petitions burnt by the hangman in May 1647. As the gulf widened between the army leaders and the Levellers he was clearly taking the part of the latter. During the Putney debates, Captain George Bishop demanded that a letter by Saltmarsh should be read in which he told the army leaders: "Ye have not discharged yourselves to the people in such things as they justly expected from ye, and for which ye had that spirit of righteousness first put upon ye by an Almighty Power."[23] When the mutinous supporters of the Agreement of the People were imprisoned and one of them shot (on 15th November), Saltmarsh was deeply moved. On 5th December he seems to have had a vision which made him believe "that the great and dreadfull day of the Lord is neere, when all men shall be judged by Jesus Christ. God [will] draw up all the sparkles of glory in one confluence to himselfe, and cause everything to returne to its first originall end." Though he lived at that time in Ilford (Essex), he determined to travel at once to the army in Windsor. There he severely reproached several high-ranking officers in the true prophetic manner, and then he informed General Fairfax "that God had revealed unto him, that he was highly displeased with his committing of Saints, and would not now prosper him. . . . The Lord . . . had of late left them, and was not in their councels, because they had forsaken him." Next he told Cromwell "that the Lord was very angry with him, for causing these godly men to be imprisoned, slighted and abused, for those Engagements which he had formerly owned." Cromwell's careful answer "that some things were not so well as he could wish" drew the milder reply from him: "I am glad . . . that there is some tendernesse of heart in you."[24] Having carried out his prophetic mission he returned to Ilford on 9th December, apparently with forebodings of death. Two days later he was in fact taken ill and died the same afternoon, consumed by the "fire in his bones."[25]

III

Saltmarsh's teaching, embodied in his beautiful writings, was of a kind that was destined to survive his own sudden death as well as the end of the Leveller movement. But it is doubtful whether he would have approved of all his later followers. Among the possible consequences of his irrational conception of the "Spirit" was a complete rejection of all learning. While the humanists merely taught that learning was not necessary for salvation, Saltmarsh was inclined "to allow Learning its place anywhere in the kingdoms of the world, but not in the Kingdom of God."[26] Saltmarsh himself, it is true, uttered a warning that nobody should be despised merely on account of being learned,[27] but it is not surprising that the uneducated among those who felt themselves transformed by the Spirit began to glory in their ignorance and to look with suspicion on all educated men. There is always something to be said for a Faustian disgust for academic scholarship after a course in "Philosophie, Juristerei und Medizin, und leider auch Theologie," but these despisers of learning rejected something of which they had but little knowledge or none at all. The consequences of this inverted snobbery were inevitable. Their lack of education, so far from freeing them from the cramping effects of merely human "notions," made some of them submit to all sorts of private dogmas and panaceas and cling to them with the stubborn fanaticism of parochial minds.

The blame for this conflict must be shared between both parties concerned. It is quite true that a good deal of university teaching was incompetent or had degenerated into theological hair-splitting, while even those who, like the Cambridge Platonists, had something important to say did very little to overcome the isolation of the universities. There was, on the other hand, a great longing among many sincere Christians for the truth of God and "the inward substantial part" of religion. Some of them, who were called "Seekers" in contemporary writings, had not been able to receive satisfaction from any of the Puritan groups. They had, perhaps, been Presbyterians, Independents and Baptists in turn, and still felt left out in the cold. Their plight was movingly described by the gentle Isaac Penington, raising his voice "out of the thick Darkness": "I can neither receive anything that is new nor return to anything that is old: but everything is darkness, death, emptiness, vanity, a lye. . . . I am weary of all things, of Religion, Reason, Sense, and all the objects that these have to converse about: but yet there is somewhat in stead of these that I would fain finde within, and somewhat . . . I would fain meet with without, which if once my spirit might be satisfied in, I should finde some rest; till when I cannot but remain truly miserable, and be fit for nothing, but to torment, and to be tormented."[28]

This intense religious yearning was, in many cases, eventually satisfied by new prophetical experiences. The prodigious crop of prophecies in the 1650's included some that were ludicrous or mad, but this should not make us insensible to the element of genuine religious power in many of them. No one who has tried to see George Fox through the eyes of his followers and friends can fail to notice the marks of what we too, in default of a better word, must call the "spirit." This applies equally to another

IAMES NAYLOR

*Of all the Sects that Night, and Errors own
And with false Lights possesse the world, ther's none
More strongly blind, or who more madly place
The light of Nature for the light of Grace.*

from Ephraim Pagitt, Heresiography, 1661
(*British Museum*)

leader of the early Quakers, *James Nayler* (1617–60), in whom this prophetic religion found its most spectacular expression.

Nayler, who described himself as a "Husbandman," was a soldier in the Parliamentary army from 1642 to 1650. Invalided out of the army, he returned home and resumed his agricultural work. It was there that he received his first message from the Lord. "I was at the Plow," he told the judges at Appleby in 1653, "meditating on the things of God, and suddenly I heard a Voice, saying unto me, Get thee out from thy Kindred, and from thy Father's House." Like Christian in Bunyan's allegory, he left wife and children. "I was commanded," he continued his evidence in court, "to go into the West, . . . [and] when I had been there a little while I had given me what I was to declare." When one of the examining magistrates remarked: "I never heard such a Call as this is, in our Time," Nayler answered with great confidence: "I believe thee."[29]

The charge brought against him at his first trial was that of blasphemy, because he was alleged to have said that Christ was in him. This in itself was merely a commonplace among the believers in the "indwelling Christ," but in his case it led to an actual identification with Christ. Nayler's appearance (he wore long hair and a beard) and his extraordinary spiritual powers made some of his followers believe that he was Christ Himself who had, at last, appeared for the second time. One of them wrote to him, "Thy Name shall be no more James Naylor, but Jesus," and some women knelt and kissed his feet. All this turned Nayler's head and he allowed his followers to stage a Messianic entry into Bristol on 24th October 1656, following the pattern of Christ's entry into Jerusalem. Nayler was on horseback, a young man led his horse, another walked in front, and some other men and women followed behind. As they went along, they sang "Holy, holy, holy, Lord God of Saba-oth."[30] So far could men be led by their trust in the super-natural influence of the Spirit upon their hearts.

During the manifold upheavals of the Puritan Revolution this kind of prophetic religion could not fail to have effects beyond the sphere of religion proper. We have already seen that John Saltmarsh was drawn into the political struggle of his day, and we shall see in some of the succeeding chapters that there were adherents of the "Religion of the Spirit" who showed such an intense concern for social justice that, in one way or another, they were bound to come into contact with public affairs. The

Christian humanists, needless to say, were not moving in the same direction. What, we may well ask, could the learned John Hales have in common with the turbulent radicalism of his contemporaries? Surely he must have counted them among those who called "their own private conceit the Spirit."[31] Yet we should be making a mistake if we were not to recognise that in his thought too there were radical potentialities. His emphasis on the spiritual equality of all believers led him to oppose the claims of the clergy that they alone had the power of admitting or refusing entrance into the Kingdom of Heaven. Everyone, he wrote, had "the keys of the kingdom of heaven committed to his power, both for his own and others use."[32] Another religious consideration suggested to him a certain conception of social equality. In his *Tract concerning Schism* he declared that social differences between men could not derive any support from Christianity or nature, "for we have believed him that hath told us, 'That in Jesus Christ there is neither high nor low,' . . . which saying cut off all claim most certainly to superiority, by title of Christianity." Inequality arose only from "agreement of men among themselves," and, we may conclude, could therefore be changed by a different agreement.[33]

This was by no means the only example known to Hales of a conflict between the standards of Christianity and the ways of the world. It applied to all secular power, "because in gaining and upholding temporal kingdoms nothing [is] so usual as the sword and war," while the Kingdom of Christ was "erected and maintained . . . not by violence, but by love."[34] This discrepancy showed itself also in economic life; "most of the bargains which the World makes," he wrote, "are copied out according to that pattern, which Judas gave at the betraying of Christ." He reminded rich men that they were at a great disadvantage concerning the salvation of their souls; they could indeed be saved, but he advised them so to live as if they could not.[35] The economic tendencies of his time were viewed by him with strong suspicion. Usury he rejected outright and deplored what he believed to be Calvin's unfortunate departure from an ancient tradition in declaring it to be lawful. "What shall we say to

God himself," he asked, "who every where decries it? What unto all good men, . . . who, for many hundred years, have still protested against it?"[36] He was, in fact, profoundly aware of the gulf between "that Christianity which is commanded unto us in the writings of the Apostles and Evangelists, and that which is current in use and practice of the times."[37]

Yet there were many reasons why Hales should have been horrified by the fanatics of spiritual religion, in spite of his sympathy with some of their aims. Hales' cultural range was unusually wide. He was equally at home in Ben Jonson's literary circle in London as in Falkland's Convivium Theologicum in Great Tew, near Oxford. He was interested in Horace as well as in St. Chrysostom, and he was among the first to recognise Shakespeare's genius. At Eton he developed a close friendship with Sir Henry Wotton, the ambassador, poet, and friend of Bacon and Donne; and Andrew Marvell considered it an honour to have known " one of the clearest heads and best prepared breasts in Christendom."[38] This urbane man could not have been expected to agree with the typical Quaker view that "Poets, Jesters, Rhimers, makers of Verses and Ballads . . . are for the undoing of many poor souls."[39] Nor could he have felt anything but dismay when another radical denounced all "Traditional Knowledge, which is attained by reading, or by the instruction of others, . . . he that only contemplates and talks . . . and doth not employ his Talents in some bodily action . . . is an unprofitable son [of mankind]."[40] Hales must have looked on all this as a grave threat to the cultural inheritance of England, as indeed it was.

Hales' attitude to social problems was therefore bound to be more complex than that of the Puritan radicals. He saw his civilisation both from within and from without.[41] He could judge it by standards transcending it and thus be aware of its limitations, but he was so intimately connected with its achievements that he was most reluctant to disturb its established institutions and traditions. To him and his friends the Civil War was an unmitigated disaster. Their interests were not represented by either side; Chillingworth's witty description of the warring parties—"Publicans and sinners on one side against Scribes and Pharisees on the other"[42]—indicates their detached position. But their complexity of thought was unlikely to have much influence at a time of open strife, when the issues were forcibly simplified. Nor do they seem to have felt a strong urge to shape contemporary affairs; if they took part in them at all, they did so only, like Falkland, to fulfil an unpleasant duty. During the Laudian régime, Hales, it is true, produced a plea for toleration, but when Laud expressed his displeasure he immediately withdrew and wrote an apologetic letter; he was not, as he knew himself, cut out for a martyr. It may perhaps be said that these humanists, like some of their predecessors of the Renaissance, showed too little zeal for reform where it was really needed; that their attachment to the established order made them neglect such ideals of liberty and justice as were implicit in their thought. They never made any attempts to realise whatever Utopia their free minds had led them to discover. Those who were determined to make such attempts can therefore hardly be blamed for going their own ways. Thus a situation arose which is all too familiar: the men with comprehensive minds were timid in action, while the courageous were narrow-minded and destructive of much that could never be replaced.

NOTES TO CHAPTER FIVE

[1] Cf. especially J. Tulloch, *Rational Theology and Christian Philosophy in England in the Seventeenth Century* (1874), i, 170–260.

[2] John Hales, *Works* (1765), ii, 94.

[3] Hales, op. cit., i, 68, 69.

[4] Tulloch, op. cit., i, 326 (cf. Hales, op. cit., iii, 69).

[5] Hales, op. cit., iii, 14.

[6] R. Cudworth, *Sermon to the House of Commons, March 31st, 1647.*

[7] Tulloch, op. cit., ii, 99.

[8] John Smith, *Select Discourses* (1660), p. 323.

[9] John Smith, "A discourse concerning the True Way or Method of attaining to Divine Knowledge," ibid., pp. 2–3.

[10] B. Whichcote, *Aphorisms*, p. 76.

[11] Cf. *D.N.B.*

[12] John Saltmarsh, *Poemata Sacra, Latine et Anglice scripta* (Cantab. 1636).

13 Woodhouse, *Puritanism and Liberty*, p. 182.

14 Saltmarsh, *Free Grace: or, The Flowings of Christ's Blood Freely to Sinners* (1645; quoted from reprint 1792), p. 207; Saltmarsh, *Sparkles of Glory; or, Some Beams of the Morning Star* (1647; quoted from reprint 1811), pp. 22, 26, 44, 228, and *passim*. Cf. Troeltsch's description of this type of religion: *The Social Teaching of the Christian Churches*, ii, 742.

15 Saltmarsh, *Some Drops of the Viall* (1646), p. 115.

16 Saltmarsh, *The Smoke in the Temple* (1646), p. 15.

17 Saltmarsh, *Some Drops of the Viall*, p. 115.

18 Cf. Saltmarsh, *Sparkles of Glory*, p. 84.

19 Saltmarsh, *Dawnings of Light* (1646), Second Preface, pp. 60, 65, 66.

20 *Reliquiae Baxterianae* (1696), p. 56.

21 Saltmarsh, *A Letter from the Army, Concerning the peaceable temper of the same* (1647), p. 2.

22 Saltmarsh, ibid., p. 1.

23 Woodhouse, *Puritanism and Liberty*, p. 438.

24 Saltmarsh, *Wonderfull Predictions Declared in a Message, as from the Lord* (1648), *passim*.

25 *England's friend raised from the Grave, being the true copies of three letters, written by Mr. John Saltmarsh, a little before his death* (1649), p. 1. For the impression made by Saltmarsh on a supporter of the Levellers, cf. Appendix B.

26 Saltmarsh, *Some Drops of the Viall*, p. 115.

27 Woodhouse, op. cit., p. 182.

28 Isaac Penington, *A Voyce out of the thick Darkness* (1650), pp. 19, 20.

29 James Nayler, *A Collection of sundry Books, Epistles and Papers* (ed. G. Whitehead, 1716), pp. 12–13.

30 Cf. W. C. Braithwaite, *The Beginnings of Quakerism* (1912), p. 252.

31 Hales, op. cit., i, 82. Cf. Henry More's rejection of the Quakers: *Conway Letters* (ed. M. H. Nicolson, 1930), *passim*.

32 Hales, op. cit., i, 96.

33 Ibid., p. 131.

34 Ibid., ii, 291, 292.

35 Hales, *Golden Remains of the Ever-Memorable Mr. John Hales* (1688), pp. 83, 84, 247.

36 Hales, *Works*, i, 200, 201.

37 Quoted by N. E. Scott, *Harvard Theological Review*, 1917, pp. 255–6.

38 Tulloch, loc. cit.

39 Humphrey Smith, *To the Musicioners* (1658), p. 8.

40 *The Works of Gerrard Winstanley* (ed. G. H. Sabine, 1941), pp. 577, 579.

41 L. C. Knights, in an illuminating essay on Ben Jonson, has pointed to such a double attitude implied in the works of that poet, where "a naïve delight in splendour is present at the same time as a clear-sighted recognition of its insignificance, judged by fundamental human, or divine standards" (*Drama and Society in the Age of Jonson* (1937), p. 187).

42 W. Chillingworth, *Sermon before Charles I at Oxford in 1643* (*Works*, 1836, p. 521).

CHAPTER SIX

GERRARD WINSTANLEY, THE DIGGER

OF all the social radicals of our period Gerrard Winstanley, the leader of the Digger movement, has attracted most attention of late. Entirely forgotten until 1895, he was rediscovered in that year by Eduard Bernstein, the well-known Marxist.[1] Since then he has been the subject of two full-length studies (by L. H. Berens[2] and D. W. Petegorsky[3]) and his works are now easily accessible in a complete edition and a fairly substantial selection.[4] It is no accident, of course, that Winstanley owes his recent fame to a Marxist: Bernstein and his successors among the Marxist historians believed that they had found in Winstanley a spiritual grandfather of Karl Marx. It will therefore be necessary, in the course of this chapter, to make a rather careful inquiry into this ancestral relation.

The known facts about Winstanley's life are tantalisingly meagre and it is extremely unlikely, after the patient researches of Petegorsky and Sabine, that any more will be discovered in the future. We know that he was a Lancashire man from Wigan, born in 1609; that his father was a trader in cloths and wool; that his education must have been limited; that he became an apprentice in London and, in 1637, a freeman of the Merchant Taylors; that he fell a victim to the economic depression of the 1640's and had to abandon his trade in 1643; and that he then moved to the country and was helped by the charity of friends. In 1648 he wrote his first pamphlet, and from April 1649 to about Easter 1650 he was engaged in establishing that little agricultural community of the "Diggers" in Surrey of which we shall have more to say in due course. Early in 1652 his last pamphlet was published; in 1660 we catch a glimpse of him living in Cobham, probably as a farmer; and then we lose sight of him.

We are much better off in regard to the workings of his mind between 1648 and 1652 when he published no fewer than seventeen pamphlets. No careful reader of these writings can fail to appreciate the intensity of his preoccupation with mystical theology and the strength of his religious experiences. Again and again he stresses his own "experimental knowledge" of religious matters, contrasting it with the mere booklearning of the clergy. Some of his tracts are, in fact, nothing else but public declarations of what the Quakers called "openings from God." He was clearly an adherent and herald of the "Religion of the Spirit." His whole theology was based on the assumption that "man has a teacher within him and this is the spirit that made the globe and lives in every creature."[5] He believed, moreover, that it was possible to be in direct and supernatural communication with this spirit, and having had some such experiences himself he proceeded to proclaim that nothing else was of any religious value at all. All "outward customes and formes" had to be abandoned. Salvation could only be found by inspiration. Clergymen were only teaching what they had learned from books and disputations, not from the "indwelling God"; they were plucking evil fruits from the "Tree of Knowledge," not from the promised "Tree of Life" which only those in whom the living God had been reborn were privileged to approach. Nobody could be saved "by believing that a man lived and died long ago at Jerusalem" or that God "was in a place of glory beyond the sun," but only by the power of God within himself.[6] It was meaningless to speak of Heaven and Hell as remote places to be seen after death without having had direct experience of them here and now: "where Hee dwels in cleare manifestations, there is Heaven"; where God is not, there is Hell. "Every Saint is a true Heaven, because God dwells in him and he in God."[7]

Like John Saltmarsh, Winstanley connected this belief in the unlimited power of the Spirit with a Joachimite conception of the millennium. He too believed that the ultimate revelation was yet to come. "The sin of the Jews," he wrote "was to keep to Moses after Christ came, and it may well be the sin of the gentiles to keep to the letter of the Apostels after God has taken up his saints into spiritual enjoyment of Himself."[7] The writings of the Apostles and Prophets, he believed, "are the report or declaration of the Gospell, which are to cease, when the Lord himself, who is the everlasting Gospell, doth manifest himselfe to rule in the flesh of sonnes and daughters."[9]

The main tendency of this "spiritual" theology is to spiritualise all ideas and events of religious significance, making use of an extensive symbolism. "Alles Vergängliche ist nur ein Gleichnis": the three Ages (each corresponding closely to the others) are only an example of the same cosmic course of events which takes place in every individual soul. The central theme is the pilgrimage of mankind towards God, and this is re-enacted over and over again in all spheres of existence. This tendency is evident in all of Winstanley's writings, and he could rely, moreover, on the contemporary "climate of opinion" which strongly favoured symbolism of all kinds. "Every man is a perfect created world," therefore the microcosm was showing the same pattern as that which "is typed out by the fabric of the great world."[10]

This all-pervasive pattern which provided the clue to all mysteries was contained in- the story of the Fall. Winstanley took the orthodox preachers to task for speaking "of a single man, called Adam, that kiled us al by eating a single fruit, called an Apple."[11] The truth was that "this Innocencie, or plaine heartednesse in man, was not an estate 6000 years agoe onely; But every branch of mankinde passes through it, and first is defiled by imaginary covetousnesse, and thereby is made a Devill; and then he is delivered from that darknesse, by Christ the restorer, and by him made one with the Father and the Son."[12] This was the plot of the cosmic drama, "this is the great battaile of God Almighty; Light fights against darknesse, universall Love fights against selfish power; Life against death."[13] Whenever selfishness entered the scene the unity of God's work was destroyed, because Love—"l'amor che muove il sol e l'altre stelle"—was the innermost bond of the universe: "the spirit of the Father . . . knits the whole creation together into a onenesse of life and moderation, every creature sweetly in love lending their hands to preserve each other, and so upholds the whole fabrique."[14]

"Universal love against selfish power"—most interpreters of the Fall would agree that this was the issue involved. But much depends on the detailed ideas about the initial state of universal love. Winstanley's theory of the recurrence of the Fall enabled him to draw on the same conceptions of classical primitivism which Walwyn had blended with his practical Christianity. Following the current view, Winstanley described the Golden Age in terms of anarchy and communism. Only self-love "forces one part of the creation, man, to be a slave to another, and thereby the spirit is killed in both"; universal love and authority were incompatible.[15] But it was, above all, the common ownership of land which he stressed as the outstanding criterion of the "Virgine-state of Mankinde." Here we are approaching the centre of his social philosophy. "In the beginning of time," he wrote in the grand biblical manner, "the great creator Reason made the earth to be a common treasury, to preserve beasts, birds, fishes, and man, the lord that was to govern this creation."[16] "The stronger did work for the weaker and the whole Earth was common to all without exception; But this singlenesse and simplicity was subject to corruption and change."[17] The Fall came through covetousness which induced men "to lock up the treasures of the Earth in Chests and houses" and thus to commit "the greatest sinne against universall Love."[18] "This particular propriety of mine and thine," runs a striking passage of his, "hath brought in all misery upon people. For, first it hath occasioned people to steal from one another. Secondly, it hath made laws to hang those that did steal."[19] Once private property is established it is always upheld by the power of the sword which "sets up one part of Mankinde, to rule over another; . . . by murder and theft, treading others under foot." "Indeed," he concluded, "this government may well be called the government of highwaymen."[20] (One is reminded of St. Augustine's famous question: "Remota justitia quid sunt regna nisi magna latrocinia?") As the two main pillars of this "Kingly power" he denounced the clergy who committed the "trahison des clercs" by providing injustice with a halo, by betraying the Spirit "into the hand of the selfish power"; and the lawyers who, under the pretence of justice, administered the will of the Conquerors and enriched themselves in the process ("The Law is the Fox, poore men are the geesse; he pulls off their feathers and feeds upon them."[21]).

Having speculated much on God and the world he was able to find rest in the allegory of the Fall and Restoration of Man. That Restoration, and with it the final scene of the divine drama, he believed to be close at hand. The old world "is running up like parchment in the fire, and wearing away," and within a few years God " wil change times and customs, and fil the earth with a new law, wherein dwels righteousness and peace."[22] Christ "shall cause men to beat their swords into ploughshares and spears into pruning hooks, and nations shall learn war no more, and every one shall delight to let each one enjoy the pleasures of the earth, and shall hold each other no more in bondage."[23] This tone of expectation is present in Winstanley's writings from the beginning, and we may assume that his entry, in 1648, into the arena of pamphlet-writers had something to do with his belief in the approaching millennium and his urge to announce it. The evidence at our disposal enables us to trace two of his attempts to contribute something towards that great event. One is the short-lived Digger community (1649–50) with which his name is primarily connected, and the other is his appeal, in 1652, to Oliver Cromwell, embodied in his pamphlet, *The Law of Freedom*.

In April 1649 we find him, together with about thirty to forty associates, digging up the commons and planting some vegetables at St. George's Hill, near Cobham, in Surrey. This was his response to an inner voice which had told him three times: "Work together, eat bread together, declare this all abroad"; the place too had been pointed out to him "by vision in dreams and out of dreams."[24] The Diggers claimed that the commons and wastes had been, since times immemorial, the property of the people as a whole and that they were therefore entitled to cultivate them as a community. This picturesque episode will always remain the most easily remembered fact about Winstanley, just as most people seem to remember that the early Quakers refused to take off their hats.[25] As in the case of the Quakers, the action of the Diggers was of a symbolical nature. The little communist group was to be a "sign of the times," a sign that the great change was about to occur. A contemporary news-sheet, hostile to the Diggers, was well informed when it asserted that the Diggers "expect a generall restauration of the Earth to its first conditions, [and] that [they] themselves were called to seek and begin this great work which will shortly go on throughout the whole Earth."[26] William Everard, the only one of Winstanley's comrades of whom we get a few glimpses, told Fairfax that the liberation of the poor was approaching and that all men would soon follow their example.[27] "Not only this common or heath should be taken in and manured by the people," wrote Winstanley, "but all the commons and waste ground in England, and in the whole world." It is only this hope which makes it intelligible that he regarded the Digger experiment as an attempt to "lift up the Creation from bondage."[28] The little community of the Diggers, joined together by love like the original Creation—

> In Cobham on the little heath our digging there goes on,
> And all our friends they live in love, as if they were but
> one[29]—

was to be the prototype of the future society, its symbolical anticipation.

Unfortunately, however, the expected support was not forthcoming. On the contrary, the local population were extremely hostile towards the Diggers from the very beginning. "The grain and vegetables the Diggers attempted to plant were time and again uprooted; their tools were smashed; houses they erected were torn down."[30] The Surrey ministers, Win-

stanley tells us, appointed a lecturer to preach against the
Diggers and incited the people to boycott them. The local
squires denounced them to the Council of State, and on 20th
April 1649 Winstanley and William Everard appeared before
Fairfax in London to clear themselves of the charges brought
against them. The central authorities did not pursue the matter
any further, but in July 1649 Winstanley and fourteen of his
comrades were arrested on a charge of trespassing and fined
ten pounds each by Kingston Court. As the Diggers were
evidently unable to pay these sums their goods were distrained.
In November the squires made use of soldiers to destroy their
houses. Early in 1650 the Diggers sent a delegation into
Buckinghamshire, Surrey, Hertfordshire, Middlesex, Berkshire,
Huntingdonshire and Northamptonshire, asking for financial
help. In the previous year a sympathetic echo had come from
Buckinghamshire,[31] and there is evidence that in Northamptonshire and Kent some attempt was made, in 1650, to follow the
example of the Surrey Diggers. That group itself, however,
came to an end in April 1650, when one of the landowners hired
some men to keep watch day and night in order to prevent
them from working on the commons. The final result was utter
failure and the shattering of Winstanley's dream.

He made one more attempt at realising it. This was, however,
of a different kind altogether. It consisted of a pamphlet containing a description of a communist society together with an
appeal to Oliver Cromwell to use his newly won power to
establish this new social system. "Now you have the power
of the land in your hand," he addressed the Protector, "you
must . . . set the land free to the oppressed commoners, who
assisted you, and paid the Army their wages; and then you will
fulfil the Scriptures and your own enjoyments, and so take
possession of your deserved honour."[32] He had addressed
Parliament in similar terms in 1649 and the first draft of the
Law of Freedom was, indeed, written in the same year,[33] the
year of the Cobham experiment. He still believed three years
later that "the Spirit of the whole Creation (who is God) is
about the reformation of the world, and he will go forward in

his work," and that the first step should be the communal cultivation of the commons and wastes of England.[34] But his appeal to Cromwell grew into something like a Utopia and presented him therefore with that particular problem which all authors of Utopias are bound to face: the problem of power.

In the *Law of Freedom* Winstanley ceased to be an anarchist.[35] Of his earlier anarchism there can be no doubt. "We . . . [are] not," he told Fairfax, "against any that would have magistrates and laws to govern, as the nations of the world are governed; but as for our parts we shall need neither the one nor the other."[36] The community of equals, the society of friends which he was envisaging, was in no need of laws and law-enforcing institutions. "For what are prisons," he wrote, "and putting others to death, but the power of the sword, to enforce people to that government which was got by conquest and sword, and cannot stand of itself, but by the same murdering power?"[37] But in his Utopia based on his social principles he had to discuss the question of how to deal with those who would not conform to these principles. He solved this difficulty by a method which planners are only too liable to adopt: offenders against the laws of the ideal Commonwealth were to be imprisoned, whipped, enslaved, or, in extreme cases, executed; the *Law of Freedom*, as in a later, more famous case, was to force everyone to be free. Forgotten was his own earlier warning: "Every one that gets an authority into his hands tyrannizes over others";[38] like many later builders of Utopias he did not apply some of his most profound social criticism to his own construction. A similar change is noticeable with regard to the related question of pacifism. Formerly he had asserted that the rule of Christ would see the end of the soldier's trade which "upholds the murderer, or the Devill."[39] Now he envisaged a popular army, not only as a safeguard against foreign invasion, but also "to beat down all that arise to endeavour to destroy the liberties of the Commonwealth."[40] He was now making a distinction between just and unjust wars: those undertaken in the cause of freedom (that is, for the principles of his social philosophy) were just.

The main economic feature of Winstanley's society was, of course, the common ownership of land. In addition, there was to be no commerce of any kind and therefore no money. Storehouses were to be established all over the country "to which all the fruits of the earth, and other works made by tradesmen, shall be brought. . . . And as everyone works to advance the common stock, so everyone shall have a free use of any commodity in the storehouse for his pleasure and comfortable livelihood, without buying and selling."[41] This depended on the assumption that "there will be plenty of all earthly commodities, with less labour and trouble than now . . . There will be no want, for every man may keep as plentiful a house as he will, and never run into debt, for common stock pays for all."[42] It is not clear how seriously Winstanley meant this, for he also wrote: "Having food and raiment, lodging and the comfortable societies of his own kind, what can a man desire more in these days of his travel? Indeed, covetous, proud and beastly-minded men desire more, either to be by them to look upon, or else to waste and spoil it upon their lusts."[43] He was probably expecting a fairly moderate standard of living to be shared by everybody.

However, Winstanley did not pretend to be an economist and we need not take him to task for being somewhat vague about the national income. He was in any case, unlike most modern socialists, thinking in terms of an association of small communities, just as he had done in his Digger days. The parish he regarded as a "bigger family," and in an attractive passage he recommended the keeping of Sunday as a day of rest so "that the people in . . . a parish may generally meet together to see one another's faces, and beget or preserve fellowship in friendly love."[44] From his administrative proposals it emerges clearly that he expected the bulk of the work to be performed by the local "peacemakers" and "overseers" and by the county courts. Although he described Parliament as "the highest court of equity,"[46] he did not specify any system of judicial appeals and he was altogether very vague about the functions of Parliament, which he charged with general supervision of the laws on behalf of the welfare of the community. Moreover, he adopted the Leveller device of the annual election, by manhood suffrage, of all public officials, including judges and members of Parliament.[46] This obviously presupposes a high degree of decentralisation. Winstanley's underlying conception of the future society was, in some ways, similar to that of the Levellers, especially as laid down in their manifesto of May 1649: the centre of gravity was to lie in the small local community, administered by its members in annual rotation, without the help of professional officials of any kind. It is therefore not surprising that Winstanley does not tackle the specific problems of modern society, which by his time had clearly made their appearance; in his society they would not have existed at all.

There is, of course, no reason why we should expect Winstanley to deal with modern social problems, except that some of his recent interpreters tend to regard him as a thoroughly modern social reformer. D. W. Petegorsky calls Winstanley "the most advanced radical of the century." C. Hill assigns to his writings a place in the series of "communist theories which have appeared with increasing maturity in all the great middle-class revolutions—Münzer, John of Leyden and the Anabaptists in the German reformation, Babœuf and the conspiracy of the equals in the French revolution, Marxist communism in 1848 and the Bolsheviks in 1917."[47] This line of succession, as well as other remarks, makes it clear that Petegorsky and Hill measure the degree of "maturity" in terms of conformity, or the reverse, with Marxist-Leninist theory (this is a well-known aspect of the particular interpretation of history which they represent). Apart from the consideration that it is somewhat difficult (and perhaps not very fruitful) to decide whether Winstanley was more of a Marxist than John of Leyden and less of it than Babœuf, this view over-simplifies matters a good deal and rests on several misunderstandings. In Winstanley's case (which alone concerns us here) it is inevitably bound up with the Marxist theory of religion. Petegorsky explains the "important revival from 1648 onwards of mystical religion and sectarian enthusiasm" by a reference to those "who, discouraged by the overwhelming resistance they encountered, despaired of realising social change through their own efforts and began, in increasing measure, to invoke the assistance of the Almighty to accomplish what political agitation had failed to achieve."[48] Winstanley is said to have outgrown this stage within a few months, to have adopted "scientific rationalism" and, early in 1649, to have "transferred his philosophical and cosmological conceptions from religion and morals to politics and economics." The fact that in 1650, after he had reached the last stage of this alleged development, Winstanley wrote a predominantly religious tract (*Fire in the Bush*) is consistently explained by his "profound disappointment at the failure of his practical venture."[49]

The evidence for Winstanley's "rationalism" is based on such passages of his as these: "The spirit that will purge mankind is pure reason. . . . It is reason that made all things and it is Reason that governs the whole Creation."[50] But the conception of *recta ratio* ("right reason") belonged to the stock of traditional theology. Winstanley was not proclaiming a startling novelty when he wrote: "The spirit of right understanding has taken up his dwelling in this flesh, and from hence man is called a reasonable creature."[51] Moreover, it is well to remember that many of the sectarian tract-writers of that period constructed a religious terminology of their own. In describing, for example, the contrast between good and evil, Winstanley used the word "knowledge" as synonymous with "good" and the word "imagination" as synonymous with "evil"; at other times he used the words "reason" (or "righteous conscience") and "flesh" to point to the same contrast.[52] In another passage the word "reason" appears among eleven names given to God.[53] It is fairly evident that Winstanley used this word for one of his manifold attempts at tracing the workings of the Spirit of God in man, and that he meant something similar to what the Quakers were to call the "Light within." It is a far cry, indeed, from such an idea to "scientific rationalism," whatever that may mean.

There is an even deeper misunderstanding implied in Petegorsky's view on the transition of Winstanley's ideas "from religion and morals to politics and economics." It amounts to a refusal to enter into ways of thought which are very remote from our own. We have separated religion and politics to such an extent that we find it difficult to imagine how it could be otherwise. But all the evidence we have suggests that no such division existed in Winstanley's mind. Already in his second (or possibly first) pamphlet, written in May 1648, he spoke of God "working out an inward and an outward peace and liberty for all,"[54] just as more than one year later, in the middle of his Digger experiment, he defined true freedom as consisting in "community in spirit, and community in the earthly treasury."[55] He believed that it is the division "within the heart of man, which is the occasion of that outward division of times,"[56] but he also knew that, once established, "the outward bondage that one sort of people lay upon another" results in "inward bondages of the mind, as covetousness, pride, hypocrisy, envy, sorrow, fears, desperation and madness."[57] Seen in this context it is not at all surprising that Winstanley wrote a religious tract in the interval between digging and writing his Utopia, and that this tract contains, in fact, some of his most radical opinions on social matters.[58]

We cannot but conclude that in this respect Winstanley, so far from being an early Marxist, shared the prevailing outlook of his time. In some other ways, however (and that adds to the interest of his writings), he seems to have anticipated views which became widespread in the later part of the seventeenth century and the early eighteenth century and have been current ever since. His symbolical interpretation of the Fall, for example, led him to the belief that every human being passes through the state of innocence, and thus to the denial of the doctrine of Original Sin: "Looke upon a childe," he wrote, "that is new borne, or till he growes up to some few years, he is innocent, harmelesse, humble, patient, gentle, easie to be entreated, not envious; And this is Adam, or mankinde in his Innocency."[59] (Hill's reference, in connection with this passage, to certain poems by Traherne and Vaughan is very much to the point.)[60] His spiritual religion, with its emphasis on the inward and complete presence of God, resulted, as we have seen above, in a certain scepticism towards traditional Christian teaching. It does not matter much, he wrote, whether there was any such outward thing as the Garden of Eden, "if thou seest all within"; and what happens to us after death he regarded as beyond our capacity to know,[61] besides being unimportant in view of the possible perfection on earth. This scepticism was growing in intensity throughout the time during which we can follow his thought and reached its climax in the *Law of Freedom*, where it is combined with his inveterate anticlericalism in the following remarkable statement: "While men are gazing up to heaven, imagining after a happiness or fearing a hell after they are dead, their eyes are put out, that they see not what is their birthrights, and what is to be done by them here on earth while they are living. . . . And indeed the subtle clergy do know that if they can but charm the people by this their divining doctrine to look after riches, heaven and glory when they are dead, that then they shall easily be the inheritors of the earth, and have the deceived people to be their servants."[62]

This might appear at first sight reminiscent of the Marxist view that religion is the opium of the people. In reality it is the most violent expression among the Puritan radicals of the anticlericalism, inspired by profound religious feelings, which we have met so often in the course of this study. Winstanley believed very strongly indeed that the existence of professional ministers of religion was not only unnecessary but highly dangerous, and as it was still the main function of Oxford and Cambridge to produce clergymen, he included the universities and, indeed, all scholarship in his condemnation. In his ideal society children were not to be "trained up only to book learning and no other employment, called scholars."[63] He was again anticipating a modern idea by drawing a distinction between "traditional knowledge, which is attained by reading, or by the instruction of others," and "practical" knowledge leading to useful occupations.[64] His educational curriculum, therefore, consisted almost exclusively of technology and science, so that "the spirit of knowledge may have his full growth in man, to find out the secret in every art."[65] But his emphasis on science was not entirely utilitarian, and there was clearly a link between his confident belief in science and his equally confident belief in the "Spirit." "To know the secrets of nature," he wrote, "is to know the works of God . . . for God dwells in every visible work or body," and he predicted that "when men are sure of food and raiment their reason will be ripe and ready to dive into the secrets of the Creation, that they may learn to see and to know God (the Spirit of the whole Creation) in all His works."[66]

It would seem, then, that the kind of spiritual religion represented by Winstanley was one of the factors changing the climate of opinion at a crucial period of European history. Some of its doctrines—notably the possibility of perfection in this life and the immanence of God in the world—were likely to support a tendency, widespread for many other reasons, towards secularisation. Its anticlericalism, besides having deep roots in the English tradition, was sure of a hearing after a protracted religious war, and its opposition to ecclesiastical dogma and its emphasis on the individual religious experience would appeal to the increasingly independent attitude of the growing secular culture at the turn of the century. Of the three persons of the Trinity, the Holy Spirit may well have seemed the least exacting and "obscurantist" to an "enlightened" age. It would not be surprising if we found that one of the forces ultimately making for the loss of religion was itself religious, though highly unorthodox, with deep roots in the religious history of Europe. However that may be, Winstanley evidently stands "betwixt and between"—a religious fanatic of the Puritan Revolution, yet anticipating something of a later intellectual atmosphere. But it is important to bear in mind that even those of his views which strike us as characteristically modern were not unconnected with his religious beliefs, which were, indeed, as far as we can gather from his writings, the mainspring of all his thought. Any interpretation tending to minimise the importance of his religious beliefs must remain unhistorical.

It would be a truism to say that Winstanley had a one-track mind; all fanatics have, and this is at the same time their weakness and their strength. When one believes oneself to have been favoured with a revelation one does not pause to consider much besides. And Winstanley's chief claim to our attention does, in fact, rest on his compelling vision of a brotherly community of peace and goodwill, on that very message which he felt to have received from the Spirit.

NOTES TO CHAPTER SIX

[References are to G. H. Sabine's edition of Winstanley's works (S.) and to L. Hamilton's *Selections from the Works of Gerrard Winstanley* (H.). All quotations are from Winstanley's writings unless stated otherwise.]

[1] E. Bernstein, *Sozialismus und Demokratie in der grossen Englischen Revolution* (1895). English translation: *Cromwell and Communism* (1930).

[2] L. H. Berens, *The Digger Movement* (1906).

[3] D. W. Petegorsky, *Left-Wing Democracy in the English Civil War* (1940).

[4] G. H. Sabine, *The Works of Gerrard Winstanley* (1941) (I am greatly indebted to the Introduction to this edition); L. Hamilton, *Selections from the Works of Gerrard Winstanley* (1944).

[5] *Saints Paradice*, p. 93 (S.).

[6] Ibid., p. 96 (S.).

[7] *Truth Lifting up its Head*, p. 114 (S.); *Saints Paradice*, p. 95 (S.).

[8] *Breaking of the Day of God*, p. 87 (S.).

[9] *Truth Lifting up its Head*, p. 122 (S.).

[10] *Saints Paradice*, p. 95 (S.); *New Law of Righteousness*, p. 17 (H.).

[11] Ibid., p. 203 (S.).

[12] *Fire in the Bush*, pp. 480–1 (S.).

[13] Ibid., p. 457 (S.).

[14] *Truth Lifting up its Head*, p. 108 (S.).

[15] *True Levellers' Standard Advanced*, p. 38 (H.); *New Law of Righteousness*, p. 15 (H.).

[16] *True Levellers' Standard Advanced*, p. 37 (H.).

[17] *Fire in the Bush*, p. 489 (S.).

[18] Ibid., p. 496 (S.).

[19] *New Law of Righteousness*, p. 24 (H.).

[20] *Fire in the Bush*, pp. 463–4 (S.); *Law of Freedom*, p. 131 (H.).

[21] *Fire in the Bush*, pp. 463, 464, 468 (S.).

[22] *Truth Lifting up its Head*, p. 121 (S.).

23 *New Year's Gift of Parliament and Army*, p. 97 (H.).

24 *True Levellers' Standard Advanced*, p. 41 (H.).

25 Saltmarsh and Winstanley, incidentally, anticipated this practice.

26 *The Kingdom's Faithfull and Impartiall Scout*, 20–27th April 1649.

27 D. W. Petegorsky, *Left-Wing Democracy in the English Civil War*, p. 163.

28 *True Levellers' Standard Advanced*, pp. 41, 40 (H.).

29 *A Watchword to the City of London and the Army*, p. 79 (H.).

30 D. W. Petegorsky, op. cit., p. 169. For an exact and detailed account of the Digger experiment and of contemporary comments on it, cf. ibid., chap. 4.

31 Cf. Chapter Four.

32 *Law of Freedom*, p. 110 (H.).

33 Ibid., p. 116 (H.).

34 Ibid., pp. 110, 114–20 (H.).

35 This has been rightly stressed by C. Hill in his introduction to Hamilton, op. cit., p. 5.

36 *Letter to Fairfax*, p. 52 (H.).

37 *Declaration from the Poor Oppressed People of England*, p. 46 (H.).

38 *New Law of Righteousness*, p. 15 (H.).

39 *Fire in the Bush*, p. 467 (S.).

40 *Law of Freedom*, p. 170 (H.).

41 Ibid., p. 179 (H.).

42 Ibid., p. 119 (H.).

43 Ibid., p. 179 (H.).

44 Ibid., p. 160 (H.).

45 Ibid., p. 155 (H.).

46 Ibid., p. 140 (H.).

47 Hill, introduction to Hamilton, op. cit., p. 4.

48 Petegorsky, op. cit., p. 115.

49 Ibid., pp. 131, 137, 148.

50 *Saints Paradice*, quoted in Petegorsky, op. cit., p. 133.

51 *Saints Paradice*, p. 95 (S.).

52 *Fire in the Bush*, pp. 452, 453 (S.); *Saints Paradice*, p. 79 (S.).

53 *Truth Lifting up its Head*, p. 138 (S.).

54 *Breaking of the Day of God*, p. 87 (S.).

55 *Watchword to City of London and Army*, p. 68 (H.).

56 *Fire in the Bush*, p. 485 (S.).

57 *Law of Freedom*, p. 123 (H.). Surely Petegorsky builds too much on this one passage, taken by itself, when he ascribes to Winstanley the Marxist notion that "human nature is primarily a product of the social conditions under which men have been living" (Petegorsky, op. cit., p. 183). This would imply that, by 1652, Winstanley had abandoned his theory of the Fall. It is quite understandable that he does not deal with it in the *Law of Freedom*, which contains the description of the restored state of mankind, but there is no reason to believe that he would have refrained from publicly revising his earlier views had he really changed his mind on such a fundamental tenet, especially in view of the publication, in 1650, of *Fire in the Bush*, in the main a treatise on the spiritual significance of the Fall.

58 Cf. quotations in this chapter from *Fire in the Bush*.

59 Ibid., p. 493 (S.).

60 Hill, introduction to Hamilton, op. cit., p. 6.

61 *Fire in the Bush*, p. 462 (S.); *Law of Freedom*, p. 163 (H.).

62 *Law of Freedom*, p. 167 (H.).

63 Ibid., p. 174 (H.).

64 Cf. Chapter Five, "The Religion of the Spirit."

65 *Law of Freedom*, pp. 174–6, 177 (H.).

66 Ibid., pp. 163, 177 (H.). There was also his insistence on "experimental knowledge" in spiritual matters, which had its counterpart in science where "everyone . . . is required to speak nothing by imagination, but what he hath found out by his own industry and observation in trial" (p. 162) (H.).

I

CHAPTER SEVEN

THE FIRST QUAKERS

MANY earnest "seekers" of the 1650's found spiritual rest in the religious community of the Quakers. This sect had sprung up in the north of England and had been carried to the south by a band of indefatigable preachers. Here, after so much uncertainty and doubt, was prophetic assurance; here, after endless wrangles about forms and ceremonies, was the pure message of the Spirit; and here, in the silence of the meeting for worship, did the Spirit speak to many who had never heard it before. Anyone reading early Quaker pamphlets, especially those written before the Restoration, must be struck by their passionate intensity. Even after almost three hundred years one can still feel the quivering emotions behind the central spiritual experience of their authors. Again and again we are told, in varying degrees of eloquence, of a transformation which George Fox was able to describe in unforgettable words: "Now was I come up in spirit through the flaming sword, into the paradise of God. All things were new; and all the creation gave another smell unto me than before, beyond what words can utter. . . . The creation was opened to me; and it was shewed me how all things had their names given them according to their nature and virtue."[1] This was Fox's most decisive "opening from the Lord" but by no means the only one. Nothing seemed more certain to him and his followers than that God was speaking directly to them in their own hearts and was guiding them out of the darkness to become "Children of Light." When Fox was beset by religious doubts, it was an inner voice that assured him that "there is a living God"; it was the Lord's command that made him take off his

shoes and cry out: "Woe unto the bloody city of Lichfield";
and even such minor matters as the refusal of the hat-honour
and the use of "thou" and "thee" were immediately revealed
to him by God. "These things," he announced, "I did not
see by the help of man, nor by the letter, . . . but I saw them in
the light of the Lord Jesus Christ, and by His immediate
spirit and power, as did the holy men of God by whom the
Holy Scriptures were written."[2] From this belief in the power
of the spirit the Quakers deduced two of their most strongly
held convictions: that only men who had such extraordinary
powers ought to preach ("to be bred at Oxford or Cambridge
was not enough to fit and qualify men to be ministers of
Christ"); and that the response to the workings of the spirit
must be purely spiritual too, that God must be worshipped in
spirit only, for He does not "dwell in temples made with
hands."[3]

The first Quakers did not escape some of the dangers inherent
in this spiritual religion. We have described above the spectacular case of James Nayler, and there were other incidents
of a similar kind. But their emphasis on direct contact with the
Spirit did not lead them, as it might well have done and as it
did others, to an aristocratic contempt for those who had not
been favoured with such contact. They were saved from this
conclusion by the absence in their theology of the Calvinist
dogma of predestination. Though they felt themselves to be
pioneers of Truth (and their belief in themselves sometimes
grew into veritable self-righteousness), they proclaimed again
and again that the Inward Light was given to "every man that
cometh into the world," and that it was their task to kindle it
in their fellow-men.

Like many other Puritans, the Quakers believed that God
manifested Himself not only inwardly in the hearts of the faithful, but also outwardly in public events. Cromwell, for instance,
was unshakably convinced, and said so again and again, that
"in every particular—in the King's first going from the Parliament, in the pulling-down of the Bishops, the House of Peers,
in every step towards that change of the Government—I say

there is not any one of these things . . . but hath an evident print of Providence set upon it, so that he who runs may read it."[4]

The Quakers were in general agreement with this kind of statement, but their interpretation of contemporary events naturally differed from Cromwell's in some important respects. It is, however, worth noting that, in spite of their pacifist tendencies, they shared the common belief of almost all anti-Royalists in the righteousness of the Puritan cause during the Civil War. The Cavaliers, maintained Isaac Penington, had sinned against God by "exalting man in an hard and arbitrary Government both over the Consciences of the upright-hearted towards God, and over the rights, liberties and persons of the Nation." At that time there had been "an honest zeal and true simplicity in the Puritans . . . which was of the Lord."[5] It was, some other Quakers added, through "the presence of the Lord" that liberty and the fundamental laws of the land had been "thoroughly vindicated and the enemyes thereof destroyed and totally subdued."[6] This view was forcefully expressed and elaborated by George Fox the Younger (Fox's namesake, junior to him "in the faith") in an interesting historical retrospect addressed to Charles II after the Restoration: "Concerning thy Father, and those that took his part, there was an eminent hand of God in breaking them down . . . [because God] saw that those that took part with thy Father were generally accounted the wisest, richest, noblest and stoutest men, and that they did glory in their Wisdom, Riches, Nobility, stoutnesse and strength, and vaunted themselves over them that were made of the same blood. He did then appear in contemptible Instruments (as to outward appearance), as in Tradesmen, Ploughman, servants and the like." The writer goes on to state that among the Puritans "there was once a tender, honest good principle, in the day when they were low; and there was true Desire in some of them after a just Liberty, both as appertaining to Conscience, and in things betwixt man and man; and they were truly sensible of many Oppressions which were in the Nation, both in matters of Religion, and in the Laws and Customs of the Land."[7] (We may note, in passing, the repeated emphasis on the close connection between religion and politics.)

The victories of the Parliamentarian army had, therefore, been acts of God. The Quaker George Bishop, who had been a Captain in the Army and had kept in touch with his former colleagues after his return to civil life, was even prepared to justify Pride's Purge and the trial of the King "for the preservation of the Publick interest,"[8] but Fox the Younger admitted to Charles II that "those in whom God did appear against thy Father . . . did act several things against you, beyond their Commission they had from God."[9] It was not, however, their rough treatment of King and Parliament which, according to the Quakers, caused the severance of the Puritans from God. That was brought about by their failure to fulfil their earlier promise to remove "all Oppressions out of the Land" and to "perfect the peoples Liberty."[10] Instead of doing this they made "themselves rich with the Nation's Treasure," while in the meantime "the Nation hath starved for want of mercy and just Judgment, . . . and the cause of the fatherless, widow and stranger, and the cause of the afflicted people have they not respected."[11] "Remember," James Nayler warned all rulers, "how it was with Oliver Cromwell, after he had taken upon him the Work of setting the Nations Free, but did it not; but instead thereof sought all ways to establish himself, and his House."[12]

After the Puritans had apostatised from their former principles they "became Great in the Earth . . . and so built and set up the same thing, in and among themselves, which they had thrown down and destroyed in another."[13] This feeling of political disillusionment was similar to that voiced by the Levellers; what had once seemed a struggle between Right and Wrong revealed itself as a mere replacement of one evil authority by another. "Some have been turned out," the Quakers complained, "and others brought into place . . . yet alas, what is there effected unto this day [1659]? What Freedom and true Liberty to subjects more than was many years ago? What Oppressions taken off from the People?" "Nothing yet but bondage and slavery is left upon them."[14] In these circumstances divine vengeance was sure to provide the last act of this drama which had begun in 1640. The events of 1659–60, culminating in the Restoration of the murdered King's son, represented to the Quakers, as to so many of their contemporaries, such a divine intervention. Fox the Younger brought his historical narrative to a close with the following words: "Then the Anger of the Lord was kindled against them; and as they forsook him, so he forsook them. . . . Then they began to divide and split amongst themselves . . . and so like Babel's builders they acted; and their Eye being blinded, they wrought their own destruction."[15]

This theological interpretation of contemporary events by the early Quakers was part of their general conception of history. The recurring pattern of historical development, as they saw it, was threefold, consisting of Golden Age, Decline, and Restoration. This pattern was, of course, suggested by the Christian drama of Paradise, Fall, and Redemption, but the classical picture of a Golden Age may have had some influence too; one of the Quakers, at least, takes it for granted when he writes: "That there was a golden time for Holiness of life and good Government before Moses had a being upon Earth, or writ his Books, . . . none that are truly wise can deny."[16] To many Quakers, however, the Golden Age was not represented by a legendary epoch but by two historical periods: by the "state of the Jews before Transgression" and by the "state of the Christians before Apostacy."[17] In those blessed days of Israel "the Judges sate in the gate, and executed judgment speedily upon the offendors, and cleansed the Land of evil-doers."[18] It was an important criterion of that excellent state of society that there were then no beggars among the Jews, and the same was true of the early Christians among whom there was "no lack nor want . . .; they that had much sold it, and gave to them that had none."[19] The Quakers believed that in the primitive state of the Christian Church purity of faith and life had reached its highest point. The reason for the decline was substantially the same as in the case of the Puritans:

the Churches "waxed fat, and were increased in treasures . . ., and then they forgot God, and rebelled against him . . ., and grew into strange Idolatries and errours."[20] Through that apostasy "the earth [came] to be subjected under the tyranny and oppression of that fourth Beast" (Daniel, vii); since then, "men have governed that ought not: and the great and rich man hath been set to rule over the poor."[21] After the dark night of Popery and slavery, early Protestantism brought a new light, if only a small one at first, and afterwards truth gradually increased in strength. Now, at last, there were signs that the final consummation of human history was about to begin.

It was quite beyond doubt to the first Quakers that the Second Coming of Christ was at hand, "the summer wherein the glory of the Lord shall be revealed unto all Nations. . . . Now is the Lord appearing, and his day dawning."[22] Even the moderate Isaac Penington was convinced that "there is indeed a great truth now held forth, that the Saints shall govern the world."[23] It is, in fact, this expectation of the approaching Millennium that provides the proper background for the social radicalism of the Quakers. Seen in its widest context of cosmic dimensions, the Millennium would mean nothing less than the undoing of the Fall. The earth would be restored "into its first purity"; all things would "be brought into their course and order again as before the fall"; and the "Man of Sin" would be overthrown.[24] The imminent doom of the world was described by the Quakers with apocalyptic fervour, in the true baroque style: "Howle, howle, shriek, yell and roar, ye Lustful, Cursing, Swearing, Drunken, Lewd, Superstitious, Devillish, Sensual, Earthly Inhabitants of the Whole Earth; Bow, bow, ye most surley Trees, and lofty Oaks, ye tall Cedars, and low Shrubs, Cry out aloud; Hear, hear, ye proud Waves, and boistrous Seas."[25] The imagination of these writers was fed by the dire prophecies of the Book of Revelation, which is abundantly quoted in many of their pamphlets, and by the traditional ideas about the Day of Judgment. "The Lord God of Power," ran one of their innumerable warnings, "is coming with Ten Thousand of his Saints, to judge the Earth, and to make a Desolation."[24] On that day the divine judgment would reverse all the established values of this corrupt world: the mighty would be put down from their seats and those of low degree would be exalted, the drama of Dives and Lazarus would be enacted again and this time on the grand scale, and thus the unmistakable prophecy of the Bible would at last come true.

According to their temperament, the Quakers concentrated on either of the two aspects of this ultimate "trans-valuation of values." It cannot be denied that in some of their utterances there is a good deal of *Schadenfreude* which is hardly compatible with Christian charity. James Nayler, for example, proclaimed with evident satisfaction: "You lustful ones, which live on the fat of the Earth . . . Dives-like, . . . you are fitted for destruction, your Day is coming."[27] Another Quaker referred mockingly to Cromwell's title "Lord Protector," and predicted: "You shall know that there is another Lord Protector whose Sword is drawn and furbished, to cut you down."[28] Isaac Penington expressed the same belief more coolly but comprehensively: "That which is high, that which is wise, that which is strong, that which is rich, that which is full, that which is fat: the Lord will lay low."[29]

The High and Mighty would come to grief, but those who had been persecuted and oppressed in body and spirit, who had been "chopped to pieces, as flesh for the pot, and ground to dust, as though they had not been God's workmanship,"[30] would have cause to rejoice. Once again it was asked: Had not Christ's Apostles been poor fishermen, and was not "Christ and those in whom he was most seene ever Pilgrims and strangers in the earth, such as you now call vagabonds?"[31] The cause of the poor and needy would now be pleaded, and for them the verdict would be contained in that almost magical word: liberty. "The captives shall come out of their captivity, and the prisoner out of the pit; and every bond-man shall be set at liberty"; God was now "breaking every yoke, and letting the oppressed go free," "both as to Civil and Spiritual Rights."[32]

"Justice and Liberty"—these, we may remember, were the

war-cries at the beginning of the revolution in the early 1640's,
and here they reappear as the hall-marks of the Quakers'
Millennium. These conceptions are, it is true, notoriously
vague, but for the Quakers they assumed a somewhat clearer
shape through their reading of the Bible. The Golden Ages of
biblical history lent their colours to the fulfilment of human
history; vision of the future and picture of the past were, as so
often, closely interwoven. The Millennium would restore the
primitive righteousness of the Jews and realise the Old Testament ideals of social justice, especially as preached by the
prophets. "Lawes and decrees," announced Edward Burrough,
"shall be changed and renewed . . . . Every yoake and burden
shall be taken off from the neck of the poor, true judgment and
justice, mercy and truth, peace and righteousness shall be
exalted, and all the Nations shall have Judges as at the first,
and counsellers as at the beginning."[33] In other respects,
mankind would resemble the Christians in the days of the
Apostles, when the fullest outward and inward liberty was
realised in a community of loving brothers; following their
example "all Nations of men may keep a Society."[34]

Though most Quakers were not opposed to the institution of
magistracy as such, some of them seem to have hoped for a
state of Christian anarchy. "Christ," wrote the youthful
James Parnel, "comes to fulfill and end all outward lawes and
government of man . . ., for as truth and righteousness growes,
the law . . . passeth away."[35] Ben Nicholson believed that "there
shall be no need of any outward law . . . but the inward law of
righteousness which the Lord will place and write in the
tables of every man's heart."[36] And George Fox was also
looking forward to a time when there would be no administration
of law; then "Country people would soon decide their businesse,
. . . this would be the way to take off oppression, this is the way
to bring the nation like a garden and a free nation, a free
people."[37] In this last passage the underlying conception of a
small self-governing community of neighbours is remarkably
similar to one of the fundamental ideas of the Levellers.

Enough has been said so far to justify the assertion that the first Quakers felt a "concern" for social justice. Looking at the world *sub specie millennii*, they found it thoroughly ripe for its impending downfall. It was a world ruled by Antichrist; "none upon earth hath bought or sold, or judged, or given evidence, or been respected . . ., that have not had the mark of the Beast."[38] This applied especially to those in authority: these Friends were deeply convinced that power corrupts. Time and again they warned their rulers to beware of "having fulnesse, of growing fat and forgetting God."[39] The condition of the powerful, wrote Penington, "hath commonly this double bad influence upon them: it blindeth their own eyes, in reference to themselves and their actions; and maketh them enemies to him who is not equally blinded with them." But the worst of it was that as soon as anyone got into a place of authority, his heart was immediately "lifted up above his brethren."[40] The most dangerous and most persistent temptation of power lay in its leading to a denial of the brotherly equality of all men.

The first Quakers' radical belief in social equality must be sufficiently stressed in order to grasp whatever they may have to say. It was not only spiritual equality that they were proclaiming, not only the conviction that the spirit might speak to anyone; they were also insisting on "equality in all things, man with man," because mankind was "made of one Blood and Mould, being the Sons of Adam by nature, and all Children of God by Creation."[41] Once again the gentlemen ("cholerick, proud, lofty-minded people"[42]) were reminded that their title had not existed when Adam delved and Eve span. Nor were the Quakers prepared to respect those who had "abundance of Earth, joyning field to field, and land to land," which they had got together by "fraud, deceit and oppression."[43] "The earth," Ben Nicholson quoted from the Old Testament, "is the Lord's and the fulness thereof, and . . . he hath given it to the sons of men in general, and not to a few lofty ones which lord it over their brethren."[44] Though the first Quakers did not make any attempts to imitate the Diggers, it seems that their sentiments were not far removed from Winstanley's.

Like so many writers who have been quoted in these pages, the first Quakers were deeply aware of the cleavage between the rich and the poor, between the "gentlemen" and the "common people."[45] There were some who were "striving to exceed one another, not scarce knowing what to invent, to eat and to drink, or to put on"; and there were others who were standing in the streets, "crying for a peece of bread."[46] "It is the poor that suffers," George Fox stated bluntly, "and the rich bears with the rich."[47] That Christians could let one another "die and starve for hunger and want," while others had too much, manifested clearly that they were Christians only in name, that they were "not members of the body of Christ."[48]

It is in the context of this radical social criticism that the specific social reforms advocated by these Friends should be discussed. All social problems would ultimately be solved only in the Millennium, but particular improvements preceding it could be considered to be "Emblems of that blessed state, which the God of glory hath promised to set up in the world."[49] Similarly, inequality and oppression symbolised that, in the widest sense of the word, "the Creation is out of order."[50] This, as we have seen, applied to economic injustice, but it was equally true of two social problems in which the Quakers, in common with other radicals, were greatly interested: the maintenance of ministers by compulsory tithes, and the existing system of law and legal procedure. It seemed to Richard Hubberthorne that covetous lawyers and priests had made "merchandize of people's souls and estates," and it was this spirit, he maintained, which had broken the peace of the nation. In a real Christian community everyone would freely "minister of his substance unto all necessary uses."[51] A refusal to pay tithes was, therefore, also a "testimony" against the satanic spirit of covetousness. Even such comparatively unimportant points as the refusal to take off the hat as a mark of social respect or the use of "thou" and "thee" to social superiors had wider implications. These attitudes were regarded by the Quakers as symbolical means of preaching the equality of all men. Only if we remember how strongly their age was permeated by symbolism shall we be able to understand the fanatical fervour with which they clung to their particular symbolical actions.[52] In their minds and in the minds of their contemporaries these demonstrations were closely connected with their central message.

The Quakers' suggestions for legal reforms were clearly meant to safeguard the interests of the poor. In their own dealings with the law they constantly suffered from the extortions of the lawyers and from the complications of the elaborate legal machinery. They demanded the reduction or abolition of lawyers' fees; the right of laymen to plead their own case in court; and the publication of all laws in English and "in a short volume, that all may know them." They also asked for guarantees against arbitrary imprisonment, and they protested against the use of capital punishment for theft and other minor offences.[53] In other ways, too, the Quakers pressed for a general improvement in the care of the poor. They often expressed their desire that there should be no beggar in England, and they prided themselves on having abolished want among the members of their own community.[54] George Fox boldly proposed that the lands of the Church and fines due to lords of manors should be given to the poor ("for Lords have enough"); John Cam suggested that "the Priests should have Storehouses, that the Fatherless children and widows might thither come and be refreshed"; and another Quaker planned a kind of labour exchange to deal with unemployment.[55]

Concerning all these reforms the early Quakers were at one with a large body of radical opinion during the Puritan Revolution. It is therefore not surprising to find that some people considered them to be dangerous opponents to the established social order. The authors of a hostile but not extravagant pamphlet viewed the Quakers' attitude to private property with suspicion, accusing them of thinking it "unreasonable that one man should have so much, and another so little," and of believing that they "are not free to be Tenants to other men." Lord Conway, writing to his steward, expressed the hope that "proprietors . . . will find better Tenants than Anabaptists and

Quakers, whose design is only to turn out the landlords"; and a Cromwellian colonel dismissed a Quaker captain who had made all the soldiers his equals, "according to the Levellers' strain."[56]

"The Levellers' strain"? Is this more than a contemporary suspicion? Some light is thrown on this question by a pamphlet of 1659, called *A Mite of Affection* and signed "E. B." Smith's *Catalogue* ascribes it to either Edward Billing or Edward Burrough, both of them Quakers, but in any case there can be little doubt from the religious parts of this work that its author was either a Quaker or very near to them in his beliefs. The political part of his programme, which he "offered to all the Sober and Free-born People within this Common-wealth," includes demands for annual parliaments, equal constituencies, annual rotation of offices, decentralisation of legal procedure, reform of prisons and poor-law, and even the abolition of "all servile Tenures or Copy-holds . . . being the badge or yoke of the [Norman] Conquest."[57] Quite a number of other Quaker tracts contain typical Leveller views. The central Leveller demand—the extension of the franchise—was put forward by George Fox the Younger, who used well-known Leveller arguments in supporting it. "The rich covetous oppressing men," he wrote, "have the only power to chuse Law-makers, and they will chuse . . . such as will uphold them in their oppression; and the poor man . . . must be subject to the Lawes which they make who are his oppressors." In this way, he added, "many thousands of men in England have been wronged of their Birth-right," although they were "farre more honest and understanding men" than those who had the vote.[58] In various other Quaker pamphlets the "just liberties of the People" and the "common civil and equal Liberty of all Men" were invoked, and Edward Burrough's *Declaration of Faith* proclaimed the sovereignty of the people by stating that "all Governors and Rulers ought to be accountable to the people."[59] Two Quakers, Anthony Pearson and George Bishop, seem to have moved in Leveller circles in the 1650's,[60] and Bishop may have had earlier connections with the Levellers as well. As a captain in the Army he took part in the Putney debates of 1647

and demanded that John Saltmarsh, the supporter of the Army
Levellers, should be heard; many years later Bishop still
praised the spirit of the Army agitators.[61] In one of Richard
Hubberthorne's tracts there is a very friendly reference to John
Lilburne's political career as a whole: it was God Himself who
had evidently "owned him in opposing many of the unjust
Powers of the Nation."[62] Fox and Nayler, too, in a passage
addressed to the Levellers, spoke highly of their aims, but they
went on to say: "You would have unity and fellowship, before
life was raised up in you."[63] In other words, Fox and Nayler
attributed the undeniable failure of the Levellers to their not
having listened to the new call of the Spirit of God (John
Lilburne, we may remember, did listen to it in the end).

Here we have the clue for answering our question. Nothing
could be further from the mind of the present writer than to
suggest that Quakerism was a political or social movement
disguised as a religious sect. It was, of course, nothing of the
kind. It was a new corporate manifestation of Christianity,
based on what were felt to be direct divine revelations. By far
the biggest part of Quaker propaganda was devoted to the
preaching of the new spiritual message; it was the spreading of
the new life-giving light that was the most pressing need, and
without it nothing could be achieved at all. At the same time,
it would be a mistake to draw a sharp dividing line between
Quakers, as religious radicals, and the social and political
radicals of their time. Such terms would be inappropriate,
because they would not do justice to the comprehensive character of the early Quaker faith. The Quakers had, indeed,
experienced the "Light Within," but what this light helped
them to see in the outer world was not very different from the
picture seen by other radicals. They believed that human
society as they found it had to be replaced by a "Society of
Friends," in a small way at first, foreshadowing the ultimate
change. Individual salvation was possible only within the
communal life of Christians on this earth, only by partaking in
the "body of Christ."

There was, however, an important difference between the

Quakers and most other radical groups with regard to the methods of pursuing their ends. This can best be illustrated by the political views of Isaac Penington, who mirrored many of the problems of his generation. He too shared a good deal of the Leveller outlook, being one of those who wanted "Universal Freedom" and "Universal, speedy, impartial Justice." He asserted that the "Right, Liberty and safety of the People consists in the Choyce of their Government . . . [and] also in enjoying the Power of altering their Government." The function of Parliament was to look after the burdens and desires of the common people and "to strike at the very root and foundation of oppression in any kind."[64] He never repudiated these views, but his particular difficulty concerned the method to be adopted in the sphere of politics. Looking at the political scene in 1650, he had to observe that the actual course of events had been brought about, and the victors made secure, by the use of force and violence; but the defeated forces too, with their plots and counterplots, had intended and were intending to use exactly the same means, and there seemed no end to it. Now the change Penington had wished to see all along was not one "of the outward form of Government, but from unrighteousness to righteousness."[65] He therefore issued a grave and profound warning not to pursue righteousness in an unrighteous way, "in such violent and irrational manner, as to make your more noble parts far worse slaves to brutish passions within, to avoid a more inferior slavery of the outward and more ignoble part."[66] Penington, it seems, had learnt from bitter experience that the means, so far from being justified by the end, have an insidious tendency to influence and distort the end; that if a thing of the spirit is fought for with material weapons it may in the process lose its very nature. Hence the Quakers' pacifism, which was their specific reaction to the general disappointment with the results of the Revolution. Not all of them were certain whether fighting was evil in all circumstances, but they seem to have been convinced that the Kingdom of God could not be advanced "by carnall weapons," nor indeed by "worldly pollicy and worldly wisdome."[67]

Unlike some other millenarians, the first Quakers were thus not trying to hasten the Second Coming of Christ by political or military action. Apart from preaching and the writing of pamphlets they could not attempt to influence the course of outward events. The turbulent years 1659–60 gave rise to high hopes, but soon after the Restoration the mirage of the Millennium faded away. It confirms the central place which we have ascribed to millenarian hopes in their social thought that after 1660 there seem to be few traces of social radicalism among them. Whether this change occurred as rapidly and completely as R. B. Schlatter suggests[68] it is difficult to say without further investigation, but about the fact itself there can be no doubt whatever. It is quite true that the Quakers now "agreed to compromise with the society about them," and it is undeniable that in the eighteenth century they "became as a body respectable and rich."[69] The first generation of itinerary prophets, on the other hand—according to a Quaker pamphlet originally "men worth three or fourscore pounds a year"[70]—had become social outcasts for the sake of their message. They were persecuted by a world the doom of which they were constantly proclaiming. Some of them might have been very poor from the outset, but none of them could have become well-to-do at a time when they were whipped and sent up and down the country as vagrants, and when they were constantly fined and imprisoned for various breaches of the law. The lives of the first Quakers are an impressive testimony to their unflagging single-mindedness.

In view of the later Quakers' compromise with society it is understandable that they tend to overlook or minimise the social radicalism of Friends before 1660. This applies, to some extent, even to the excellent works of the Quaker historians W. C. Braithwaite and R. M. Jones, who are inclined to present the Quaker tradition in too unbroken a line. Yet there is surely no need for Friends to be ashamed of the social teaching of their ancestors. Together with many of their contemporaries they showed a deep desire for the establishment of the "good society," and they were fully aware of the religious nature of this task. The Kingdom they heralded was not *of* this world, but it was to be set up *in* this world, and its King was therefore this world's rightful judge.

NOTES TO CHAPTER SEVEN

1 George Fox, *Journal* (Everyman's edition), p. 17.

2 Ibid., pp. 15, 39, 6, 22, 20.

3 Ibid., p. 6.

4 Speech on 14th July 1653.

5 Isaac Penington, *Some few Queries and Considerations Proposed to the Cavaliers* [n.d., but evidently after 1660], p. 1; *An Answer to that common Objection against the Quakers, That they condemn all but Themselves* (1660), p. 2.

6 George Bishop and others, *The Cry of Blood* (1656), p. 140.

7 George Fox the Younger, *A Noble Salutation and a Faithful Greeting unto Thee Charles Stuart* (1660), pp. 5, 6.

8 George Bishop, *Mene Tekel* (1659), pp. 45, 37.

9 George Fox the Younger, *Noble Salutation*, p. 6.

10 Ibid., p. 7; Richard Hubberthorne, *A Word of Wisdom and Counsel to the Officers and Souldiers of the Army in England* (1659). (*A Collection of the several Books of Richard Hubberthorne* (1663), p. 236.)

11 Edward Burrough, and others, *A Declaration from the People called Quakers* (1659), pp. 3–4.

12 James Nayler, *A Warning to the Rulers* (1659). (*A Collection of Sundry Books, Epistles and Papers, written by J. N.* (1716), p. 760.)

13 George Fox the Younger, *Noble Salutation*, p. 7.

14 Edward Burrough, and others, *Declaration from the Quakers*, p. 10; Richard Hubberthorne, *Collected Works*, p. 235.

15 George Fox the Younger, *Noble Salutation*, p. 8.

16 Martin Mason, *Innocency cleared* (1660).

17 George Fox, *To the Protector and Parliament of England* (1658), p. 12.

18 Richard Hubberthorne, *The Real Cause of the Nations Bondage and Slavery* (1658 [?]). (*Collected Works*, p. 221.)

19 George Fox, *To Protector and Parliament*, p. 12; Edward Burrough, *The True State of Christianity* (1658), p. 11.

20 Edward Burrough, *A Measure of the Times* (1657), p. 5.

21 Edward Burrough, *To the Parliament of the Commonwealth of England* (1659), p. 2; cf. also Burrough, *A Measure of the Times*, p. 21.

22 Ibid., p. 21 (cf. countless other passages in early Quaker pamphlets).

23 Isaac Penington, *A Considerable Question about Government* (1653), p. 7. Penington did not join the Quakers until 1657 or 1658, but he had been approaching their faith for some years before that.

24 Francis Howgill, *The Measuring Rod of the Lord* (1658), p. 25; George Fox, *An Instruction to Judges and Lawyers* (1657), p. 8; George Bishop, *A Tender Visitation of Love to both the Universities Oxford and Cambridge* (1660), p. 16; George Fox the Younger, *England's Sad State and Condition Lamented* (1661), p. 7.

25 Edward Billing, *An Alarm to All Flesh* (1660), p. 1.

K

[26] Francis Howgill, *A Warning to all the World* (1660). (*Collected Works* (1676), p. 26.)

[27] James Nayler, *A Call to Magistrates, Ministers, Lawyers, and People to Repentance* (1652 [?]). (*Collected Works*, pp. 135–6.)

[28] James Parnel, *A Collection of the Several Writings* (1675), p. 465.

[29] Isaac Penington, *The Way of Life and Death* (1658), p. 66.

[30] F. Howgill, *The Measuring Rod*, p. 25.

[31] E. Burrough, *A Measure of the Times*, p. 5; James Nayler, *A Salutation to the Seede of God* (1665), p. 37.

[32] Humphrey Smith, *An Alarum Sounding forth unto all the Inhabitants of the Earth* (1658), p. 8; George Fox the Younger, *A Few Plain Words* (1659), p. 4; John Crook, *The Epistle of Love* (1660), p. 17.

[33] Edward Burrough, *A Measure of the Times*, pp. 33–4.

[34] George Fox, *An Instruction to Judges and Lawyers*, p. 29.

[35] James Parnel, *A Shield of Truth* (1665), p. 20.

[36] B. Nicholson, *Some Returns to a Letter* (1653), p. 7.

[37] George Fox, *Fifty-nine particulars laid down for regulating things* (1659).

[38] Edward Burrough, *A Measure of the Times*, p. 30.

[39] George Fox, *To Protector and Parliament*, p. 14.

[40] Isaac Penington, *The Fundamental Right, Safety and Liberty of the People* (1651), address to Parliament; *A Considerable Question about Government* (1653).

[41] George Fox, *To Protector and Parliament*, p. 14; *The Royal Law of God Revived* (1671–2).

[42] Richard Farnworth, *Cesars Penny to be paid by Cesars Friends* [n.d.], p. 4.

[43] George Fox, *To all who love the Lord Jesus Christ* (1653), p. 10; James Parnel, *A Trumpet of the Lord Blowne* (1655), p. 1.

[44] B. Nicholson, *A Blast from the Lord* (1653), p. 10.

[45] J. Parnel, *Shield of Truth*, p. 21.

[46] George Fox the Younger, *The Dread of God's Power* (1660), p. 4.

[47] George Fox, *Instructions to Judges and Lawyers*, pp. 27–8.

[48] Edward Burrough, *The True State of Christianity*, p. 11.

[49] Isaac Penington, *Somewhat Spoken to a Weighty Question* (1661), p. 4.

[50] Richard Hubberthorne, *Collected Works*, p. 219.

[51] Ibid., p. 222.

[52] "A spectacular symbolical action was performed in 1654 by the religious fanatic Thomas Taney who 'lighted a bonfire, into which he threw a Bible, a saddle, a sword, and a pistol, telling those who crowded round the exhibition that these were the Gods of England '" (S. R. Gardiner, *History of the Commonwealth and Protectorate*, iii, 235).

[53] George Fox, *Instructions to Judges and Lawyers*, pp. 29, 20; James Nayler, *An Account from the Children of Light* (*Collected Works*, p. 616); George Fox, F. Howgill, R. Hubberthorne, and three others, *For the King and Both Houses of Parliament* (1661), p. 7; George Fox, *To Protector and Parliament*, p. 14; John Cam, *Some Particulars concerning the Law* (1655), p. 2; Edward Burrough, *Declaration from the Quakers*, pp. 6–7.

[54] George Fox [?], *To the Council of Officers* [n.d.], p. 5.

[55] George Fox, *Fifty-nine particulars*; John Cam, *Particulars*, pp. 2, 4; W. C. Braithwaite, *Second Period of Quakerism*, p. 559.

[56] John Pomroy, Paul Glisson, Joseph Kellet, *A Faithful Discovery of a Treacherous Design of Mystical Antichrist* (1653), p. 24; *Conway Letters*, ed. M. H. Nicolson (1930), p. 161 (Letter of 5th July 1659); W. C. Braithwaite, *The Beginnings of Quakerism* (1912), p. 520 (cf. also Richard Blome, *The Fanatick History* (1660).

[57] E. B., *A Mite of Affection* (1659), points 6, 8, 9, 14, 18, 19, 27, 29.

58 George Fox the Younger, *A Few Plain Words*, pp. 2, 3.

59 John Crook, *Epistle of Love*, pp. 12–13; George Bishop, and others, *Cry of Blood*, p. 138; F. Howgill, *Collected Works*, p. 332; Edward Burrough, *Declaration of Faith*, p. 7.

60 S. R. Gardiner, *History of the Commonwealth and Protectorate*, iii, 228.

61 Woodhouse, *Puritanism and Liberty*, p. 81; George Bishop, *Mene Tekel*, p. 46.

62 R. Hubberthorne, *Collected Works*, p. 83.

63 George Fox and James Nayler, *A Word from the Lord, unto all the faithless Generation of the World* (1654), p. 13.

64 Isaac Penington, *A Voyce out of the Thick Darkness* (1650), Preface; *The Fundamental Right, Safety and Liberty of the People* (1651), pp. 1, 3, 5, 9.

65 From a letter, quoted by J. G. Bevan, *Memories of the Life of Isaac Penington* (1807), p. 7.

66 Isaac Penington, *A Voyce out of the Thick Darkness*, Preface.

67 Edward Burrough, *Measure of the Times*, p. 34.

68 R. B. Schlatter, *Social Ideas of Religious Leaders 1660–1688* (1940), Appendix III.

69 Ibid., p. 235.

70 George Fox [?], *To the Council of Officers*, p. 5.

CHAPTER EIGHT

THE MONARCHY OF CHRIST

MANY of us may have thought at one time or another: "If only a handful of honest and just men were given the task of governing: how soon they could set the world right." There was a time during the Puritan Revolution (from July to December 1653) when it seemed as if precisely this wish had come true. Having dismissed the Rump in April 1653, Cromwell asked the sectarian congregations all over the country to suggest members for a new representative body. Out of these, together with some others, the Army Council chose 140 men to be summoned to Whitehall. Many of them deserved to be called, as they were in the summons, "persons fearing God and of approved fidelity and honesty." On 4th July they were addressed by Cromwell who told them enthusiastically: "Truly God hath called you to this work by, I think, as wonderful providences as ever passed upon the sons of men in so short a time."[1] On the following day they assembled at 8 a.m. "to begin with seeking God by prayer. . . . The service was performed by the members amongst themselves, eight or ten speaking in prayer to God, and some briefly from the word, much of the presence of Christ and of his spirit appearing that day, to the great gladding of the hearts of many."[2] This prayer-meeting lasted the whole day, until 7 p.m.

After these solemnities the new members of Parliament settled down to business. Their predominant interests are indicated by their choice of committees: in addition to the inevitable committees for the army and for Scottish and Irish affairs, they set up committees for prisons and prisoners, for law reform, for poor relief (this was later asked to report also about enclosures), for public debts, and for tithes. A strong concern for social reform is clearly evident from the outset. Soon it appeared, however, that two parties were facing each other: a group of Moderates numbering about eighty, and a group of Radicals consisting of about sixty members and thus presenting a sufficiently important challenge to the majority. The conflict centred round two controversial issues which we have several times come across in this study: tithes and law reform. Only a few days before this Parliament assembled a Puritan group in Kent had petitioned Cromwell to abolish tithes and to "regulate the law, and abolish all Statutes, Acts and Ordinances which are oppressive, and opposite to that just rule and good word of the most high." These Kentishmen further declared, echoing the radical Levellers, that certain classes of men should be held incapable of ruling the country, because they were notorious oppressors: lawyers, impropriators, lords of manors and "the Rich that is covetous: for he regardeth not the cryes of the Oppressed . . . corrupting himself with the gain of this world, making it his only felicity, not regarding God nor godliness."[3] Whether this was a representative view it is difficult to say, but the only surviving account of this Parliament from the radical point of view does contain similar references. Many laws, according to this anonymous author (perhaps Samuel Highland, a Baptist), had been made "in favour of kings, and the lusts of great men" and were therefore incongruous "with the word of God and right reason." The same applied to old lawsuits used as precedents, for "who knoweth whether in these cases bribery did not make the judgment, or the powerfulness of some great men, or the love or hatred of the judge, or the negligence and corruption of the advocate?" Concerning the question of property (the radical members were, of course, suspected of being communists) this writer proclaimed that Parliament could take away property "when particular men's property is prejudicial to common good"—a sufficiently elastic doctrine to explain some of the fears of the Moderates.[4]

It has often been asserted that the members of this "Parliament of Saints," as it is sometimes derisively called, were of low social origin. This, however, is certainly not the case. "The larger proportion of the nominees . . . were men of public reputation and of good standing in Society, old Parliamentarians, lawyers, soldiers and country gentlemen."[5] It is interesting to note that Sir Anthony Ashley Cooper (the future Lord Shaftesbury, Dryden's "Achitophel") and George Monck sat in that House. Among the more pious members were such respectable men as the well-to-do Baptist leather-seller Praise-God Barebone (whose picturesque name posterity associates with this Parliament); Samuel Moyer, a Baptist with a great financial reputation; and Francis Rous, the mystical writer and Provost of Eton. Nor can it be said that the Radicals showed a different social composition from the Moderates; members of the higher classes were evenly distributed in both groups. The social classes which had always prevailed in Parliament were again predominantly represented, but many of the men selected by the Puritan sectarians of 1653 differed greatly, in religious outlook and social concerns, from their predecessors who had been elected to the Long Parliament. A similar gathering could not, indeed, have been convoked in 1640. Since then much had happened, and the religious currents among the common people had penetrated far beyond their originally limited sphere.

The immediate programme of the Radicals amounted to this: (1) the abolition of all tithes and support of the ministers by voluntary contributions from their congregations; (2) the abolition of the notorious Court of Chancery (it was said that 23,000 cases were pending there), the reduction of all laws "into the bigness of a pocket book," and the reform of legal procedure in such a way that "any ordinary cause might be determined and ended for twenty or forty shillings, and in a very short time."[6] The Radicals have often been ridiculed as unpractical dreamers, and it is true that they were, for instance, so eager to destroy the Court of Chancery that they did not make any provision for the disposal of the outstanding cases. But there is no reason to assume that these men, given time and opportunity, would not have learned to deal with practical affairs. Some of their aims were, indeed, quite within the limits of practical politics. The abolition of tithes was by no means impossible, and a thorough reform of the law was certainly overdue; in both cases much later trouble would have been avoided. What other reforms might have followed we do not know for certain; we shall see presently that the hopes of some ran high indeed. But the Moderates, supported by the Army leaders, were not prepared to wait for further developments. On 12th December a substantial number of Moderates came to the House unusually early, and, in the absence of many of their opponents, they moved and carried the dissolution of the Assembly. The Speaker, who was in the conspiracy, and the victorious majority left the House. A minority of about thirty members remained behind and had to be dispersed by the threat of force. Once again absolute power was in the hands of the Army leaders.

Thus, according to a friend of the Radicals, "the glorious cause of Christ [was] betrayed by its pretended friends."[7] If we want to discover the full meaning of this remark, we too must leave the House of Commons and go to St. Anne's, Black-friars. This was the centre of a sect which had gathered round a few prominent Puritan preachers. Among the members of this sect, generally known as the Fifth Monarchy Men, were a number of soldiers and ex-soldiers; the most outstanding was Major-General Thomas Harrison, who also sat in Barebone's Parliament. The Fifth Monarchy Men based their beliefs on an interpretation of the seventh chapter of Daniel (together with other prophecies of the Old Testament). The four beasts were the four great empires of history: the Babylonian, the Persian, the Greek and the Roman. The Fourth Monarchy had been shaken to its foundations in 1649 with the beheading of Charles I and was due to be replaced, within the next few years, by the Fifth, the Monarchy of Christ. This doctrine was powerfully preached at Blackfriars and had got hold of some (not all, it should be added) radical members of Barebone's Parliament; on one occasion a vote could not be taken because too many members were "praying at the Blackfriars."[8] The Fifth Monarchy Men seem to have hoped that this Parliament

would help "to make straight the way of the Lord." After this
dream had been shattered, some of them even attempted armed
risings against the Government, which in each case were easily
suppressed.[9] But here we are principally concerned with the
question: How did the prophets of Christ's Monarchy envisage
their coming Jerusalem?

Once again one should beware of over-simplification. Not
all Fifth Monarchy Men had exactly the same mental picture
of the Millennium. One trend of thought can best be studied
in the writings of William Aspinwall, one of the Fifth Monarchy
pamphleteers. Here we can watch the workings of a narrow
and unimaginative mind. To Aspinwall, mankind was un-
bridgeably divided between the chosen few and the sinful
multitude [10] Not content, however, with eternal bliss, the Elect
were to be the élite on earth. Whether directly under Christ,
or in His absence, the Saints were to "exercise and manage . . .
[the] supremacy of power"; they were to be, as he put it in
a revealing and almost ludicrous phrase, "the Lamb's Military
Officers." It would fall to the Saints alone to appoint their
deputies in every city, and these, in their turn, would fill all
other public posts.[11] The Saints themselves would be either
"Judges, Clerks, Collectors of Customs and Tributes, and
Treasurers," or Overseers whose duty it would be to control
the other officials, "to call them to account, and censure them
according to their merit." There would be no other laws
apart from those contained in the Bible "which though they
be few and brief, yet are they compleatly sufficient and perfect."
Some of the consequences of this sweeping statement are
appalling: Aspinwall rejects, for instance, the institution of the
jury because there is not one word about it in the Scriptures,
nor does he allow any appeal against a judgment of the Saints
"because that would be a dishonour to Christ." His criminal
code prescribes the capital punishment for twelve offences,
among them adultery, "wilful profaning the Sabbath," and,
most ominously, "cursing the Rulers of the people."[12] He
was evidently prepared to set up an elaborate machine of
government, both civil and military, for the dictatorship of the

Saints. He did, it is true, mention a final stage when the Saints would beat their swords into ploughshares, but, like some later millenarian fanatics, he was much more interested in developing his state machine than in its withering away. We cannot help feeling that he was right in considering this Monarchy "dreadful and terrible to carnal men"; men of flesh and blood would have found it utterly intolerable.

In the cases of some other Fifth Monarchy Men it is not so easy to know how they envisaged the Millennium, but something can be gathered from their interest in contemporary social evils. The radical members of Barebone's Parliament, as we have seen, were particularly concerned about the state of the law and the abolition of tithes, and lawyers and clergymen were indeed the constant targets for the social criticism of the Fifth Monarchy Men. According to Christopher Feake, they were, together with the soldiers, the "grand tyrants of the nation."[13] John Rogers too, the most learned and perhaps the most influential preacher of this sect, mercilessly attacked these two professions, which, it seems, had a symbolical significance for him, beyond their proper sphere of action. The lawyers in Parliament, he thought, had "hindered the Reformation" by deflecting the desire for religious renewal into the channels of worldly policy. The lawyers, "the tyrants and oppressors of the civil state," corresponded to the priests who were "the tyrants and oppressors of the Ecclesiastical state." Both lawyers and priests were "greedy devourers, insatiable for covetousness, always desiring, but never delighting to work, sow, labour, nor plough, but to eat up the fruits of other men's labour, and to . . . take possession of the best meadows, vallies and pleasant places of the land." In short, together they were the two foremost types of Antichrist's subjects: his laity and his clergy.[14] (It is not quite clear what Rogers meant by "priest": probably any minister of religion who was not supported by the voluntary contributions of his congregation.) It would be easy to multiply these examples from other writings of the Fifth Monarchy Men. Here it may suffice to mention Dr. Peter Chamberlen's dry question concerning lawyers' fees:

"Whether he that must deliver his Purss upon the High Way, or he that must deliver the best part of his Estate in a private Study have the better choice?"[15]

But these men did not confine their attacks to lawyers and clergymen. We can discover among them the same general suspicion of "great men" which we have traced among the radical Levellers. Rogers' commentary on the commandment "Thou shalt not steal" ran: "There are great thieves and little thieves (great ones are now in present Powers)."[16] "You are to understand," Feake assured his readers, "that the Supream Powers have always, in all Ages, ruled partly like men, and partly like wilde beasts."[17] "What is become of all their declarations, protestations and professions?" asked Vavasor Powell, a fiery Welsh preacher of the Fifth Monarchy, "are they choked with lands, parks, and manors?"[18] Behind all this was a strong belief in social equality, for "what do Priviledges signifie, saving thou shalt not Steal, but I may?"[19] There must be, proclaimed another millenarian, the same law and liberty for everyone, for the poor as for the rich: "or it is not a Commonweal."[20] Dr. Chamberlen, the busy reformer and sharp critic, enforced his social criticism by a detailed scheme for a new system of poor relief. Like Samuel Chidley, he was particularly concerned about the arrears of pay of the soldiers, who were forced to sell their debentures at a fraction of their nominal value. He suggested the forming of a joint stock company which would be financed initially by the lands confiscated from King, Church, and Royalists, and which could, he thought, provide work for 200,000 people, thus raising them from the status of paupers to that of useful citizens. (The work would have included the reclaiming of land and the reopening of disused mines.) "The most necessary work of mankind," he wrote, "is to provide for the poor," and he addressed Parliament in a menacing tone: "Provide for the poor, and they will provide for you. Destroy the poor and they will destroy you. And if you provide not for the poor, they will provide for themselves."[21]

Men like Aspinwall did not, of course, believe in any sort of

equality; the difference between the Saints and the sinful crowd
had to find its expression in the institutions of the Fifth
Monarchy. Wherever this tendency prevailed among millenarians (and it was a possible consequence of Calvinist
dogma), democracy was sharply rejected. Hence, at Putney,
the opposition of men like Thomas Harrison to the Agreement
of the People, or the opinion put forward by the millenarian
preacher William Erbury: "I do think that a dozen or twenty-
four may in a short time do the Kingdom as much good as four
hundred that sit in the Parliament in seven years."[22] It was this
attitude, too, which suggested the entirely unconstitutional
principle of selection for the Barebone Parliament. But here
we must take into account the view expressed by the spokesman of the Radicals in that Parliament that they did not wish
to deny the people's "just right and dearly purchased liberty"
to elect their own representatives, and that they meant to take
charge of public affairs for one year only.[23] That this was not
an afterthought intended to win popular favour for the dissolved
Parliament is borne out by John Rogers' *Epistle to Cromwell*,
dated 3rd June 1653 (i.e. before the Parliament had assembled),
where he suggests that there should be "a yearly election
(or so) of officers in greatest trust or power, least they should
in time assume an absoluteness to themselves, and become
oppressors."[24] If there had been no democrats in that assembly
it would be difficult to understand that the case of John Lilburne
(who had returned from exile without being pardoned) was one
of the issues which divided the House, many of the Radicals
showing sympathy for the Leveller leader.[25] Later, too, John
Rogers was pleading for a popular government; he did, indeed,
go so far as to imply that such a government was necessary in
a Christian Commonwealth.[26] Some of the members and
followers of this sect, we may sum up, had a share in the contemporary aspirations towards social equality and democratic
rule; they refused to draw Aspinwall's terrifying conclusions
from their common belief in the mission of the "Saints." But it
is evident that the Quaker belief in a divine "Spirit" potentially
accessible to all men was a securer basis for egalitarian views.

The Fifth Monarchy Men were fiercely attacked in their own time and ridiculed by posterity, and both these reactions are intelligible. But the Barebone Parliament should not be made to suffer for all the shortcomings of the preachers at Blackfriars; it deserves a better name in history. And there is something in the character of men like John Rogers that cannot but command our respect. We get a particularly enlightening glimpse of him in his conversation with Oliver Cromwell in 1655, when he was pleading for his release from imprisonment. He declared that the Protector had "a worldly interest which God would destroy," whereupon Cromwell retorted: "Ha! And do you judge me?" Here is Rogers' torrential answer: "Yea, by the word of the Lord, in the majesty, might, strength, power, vigour, life, and authority of the Holy Ghost I can, do, and dare judge you and your actions."[27] The courage, at least, of these redoubtable soldiers of the Lord is beyond doubt.

NOTES TO CHAPTER EIGHT

[1] Cromwell, Speech on 4th July 1653.

[2] *An Exact Relation, Somers Tracts*, vi, 269.

[3] *No Age like unto this Age . . . Being the cries in Kent against the Great Oppression of Tythes, unjust Justices, and corrupt Magistrates* (1653; Thomason's date: 24th June), pp. 13, 22.

[4] *Exact Relation, Somers Tracts*, vi, 277, 278, 280.

[5] H. A. Glass, *The Barebone Parliament* (1899), p. 62.

[6] *Exact Relation, Somers Tracts*, vi, 275, 276, 278.

[7] Christopher Feake, *A Beam of Light* (1659), p. 57.

[8] *Exact Relation, Somers Tracts*, vi, 273.

[9] For a full account cf. L. F. Brown, *The Political Activities of the Baptists and Fifth Monarchy Men* (1912).

[10] The minute-book of a Fifth Monarchy congregation in Lothbury, London, opens with the formidable entry: "Delivering to Satan for Fornication," followed by the name of the offending member. (Rawlinson MSS., D 828, fol. 3, Bodleian Library.)

[11] William Aspinwall, *A Brief Description of the Fifth Monarchy . . . that shortly is to come into the World* (1653), pp. 4, 5, 6, 9.

[12] William Aspinwall, *The Legislative Power is Christs Peculiar Prerogative* (1656), pp. 26, 30.

[13] Rawlinson MSS., A 26, fol. 240.

[14] E. Rogers, *Some Account of the Life and Opinions of a Fifth Monarchy Man* (1867), pp. 39, 87.

[15] Peter Chamberlen, *Legislative Power in Problems* (1659), p. 6.

[16] E. Rogers, op. cit., p. 204.

[17] C. Feake, *The Oppressed Close Prisoner in Windsor Castle* (1655), p. 3.

[18] Domestic State Papers, vol. xlii, 20th Dec. 1653; cf. *A Declaration of several of the Churches of Christ* (Thomason's date: 2nd Sept. 1654): "Did we ever think to see so many hopeful Instruments in the Army, Churches, and elsewhere to be so fully gorged with the flesh of Kings, Captains, and nobles, etc. (i.e. with their Lands, Manors, Estates, Parks, and Palaces) so as to sit with ease and comply with Antichrist, the World, Wordly Church, and Clergie?"

[19] P. Chamberlen, *Legislative Power*, p. 4.

[20] John Brayne, *The New Earth, or, The True Magna Charta of the past Ages, and of the Ages or World to come: called the Jews Commonweal* (1653), p. 24.

[21] P. Chamberlen, *The Poor Man's Advocate* (1649), *passim*.

[22] Woodhouse, *Puritanism and Liberty*, p. 173.

[23] *Exact Relation, Somers Tracts*, vi, 269.

[24] E. Rogers, op. cit., p. 53.

[25] Thurloe State Papers, i, 387; *Exact Relation, Somers Tracts*, vi, 271.

[26] J. Rogers, *A Christian Concercitation with Mr. Prin, Mr. Baxter, Mr. Harrington* (1659), p. 121.

[27] E. Rogers, op. cit., p. 197.

CHAPTER NINE

MORE REFORMERS AND CRITICS

NOT all of the numerous men who published their views on social reform in this period can be or deserve to be mentioned here. Among them were the notorious possessors of an *idée fixe*, tormented by it, and in turn tormenting others, and those who were only echoing what can be heard more clearly elsewhere. But a brief consideration of a few more "obscure men" may serve to round off this study and to amplify some of its results.

There is, first of all, a certain *Mr. Samuel Herring* of Swan Alley in Coleman Street, London, who wrote a long letter, preserved among Cromwell's papers,[1] to the members of Barebone's Parliament. Mr. Herring, it appears, was a mystic and a disciple of Jakob Böhme, the Silesian shoemaker, whose works were translated into English from 1645 onwards and who had an enthusiastic band of adherents in England. Like Winstanley and the Quakers, Herring had extraordinary mystical experiences: "Sinkinge down into humility in selfe annihilation, I was led by the noble mind into the true nothing, in which the vanity of all things did appear unto me, which caused such exulting joy and ravishment of spirit, that I earnestly wished for the dissolution of my outward body." This "annihilation of self" could only be achieved by intense contemplation. Herring therefore suggested that two colleges in each university should be set apart "for such as shall wholly and solely apply themselves to the studdy of attaining and enjoying the spirit of our Lord Jesus" with the help of the Bible and the works of Böhme and other writers "who had true revelation from the true spirit." It is interesting to note this desire of an extreme Protestant for the re-establishment of something like a contemplative order, a Little Gidding for mystics; not even the Quakers seem to have felt the need to withdraw from the world to the same extent.

Once again, however, we find that mystical withdrawal from the world can go together with, and indeed inspire, a lively interest in social justice. A certain conception of social equality was inherent in Herring's emphasis on contemplation, "for God is noe respecter of persons, and in the true selfe annihilation, the poorest is as acceptable to him, as the greatest and richest Prince." This, of course, is the religious version of Rainborough's famous formula about the "poorest he" and the "greatest he," but Herring was not content with proclaiming it in that sphere alone. He insisted that "poore understandinge men, of good lives and conversations, having a sound rationall part, may as well be chosen to publique places of trust, as the rich knaves and fools of the outward world." He pleaded further that "the tytles of Duke, Marquess, Earle, Lord, Knight, Esquire, and such like should be layd asyde, as a vaine glorious thinge; for God's people should be under but one name, viz. Christians, or for distinction in the Commonwealth, Freemen of England." Nor was he unaware of the importance of economic inequality. The poor, he demanded, should be supported out of public funds created by the sale of all church lands, "soe that none should be found begging in the streets of our Israell, but that houses should be bought in citty, towne and countrey for old people to be cherished in, and fitted for heaven, and for young people to be brought up to worke in." The necessary work involved in the erection of these Poor Law Institutes should be performed by "the rich knaves and fooles of the outward world . . .; for, as they . . . doe compell their inferiors to assist them in raking together the muck of this world, so [Parliament] . . . should compell them to assist . . . in bringing about the worke of God." Similarly, he wanted to abolish all taxes that were "burthensome to the meaner sorte of people"; all necessary expenses of government were to be borne by the rich. Of Herring's other reforming ideas only one interests us here, concerning law. He added his voice to the chorus of those who demanded "that every shire should have its own naturall privilege in decydinge all differences betwixt party and party" and that people should not "be troubled to come to London to spend their tyme and estates." Matters of small importance should not be taken to court at all, but should be decided by the neighbours. In this way, "true simple justice" could be "erected at every man's gate," and then, as he put it in a vivid and illuminating phrase, there would be no need of "lordly judges to ride circuits, to frighten people with their bloody robes, state and pompe."

Such was Samuel Herring's message, delivered at a time which must have seemed auspicious to its author. Six years later, in 1659, similar letters were sent to Parliament by a man who had come over to England from his native Holland for this very purpose: *Peter Cornelius van Zieriksee*.[2] We know nothing of Cornelius' early life. According to his own account, his spirit was much troubled by seeing that "policy and religion (which ought to be universal) was divided and severed into many sects," and when he looked round to find where one could begin to rectify this evil, he decided that it was most hopeful to approach Oliver Cromwell. (This is an interesting sidelight on Cromwell's reputation in certain circles abroad.) He travelled to England, probably in June 1658,[3] and was several times received by the Protector, and "heard . . . with patience." It seems that he embodied his message in two letters, which he proceeded to publish after Cromwell's death, for the attention of the new Parliament. From these letters, and a subsequent pamphlet published a few months later, Cornelius emerges as a latitudinarian of John Hales' and William Walwyn's kind. His English style is, indeed, quite close to Walwyn's, and it is not impossible that he was helped by Walwyn or a man of a similar outlook; it is unlikely that his command of English would have been sufficiently great to enable him to write these pamphlets without any aid from a native Englishman. Like Walwyn, Cornelius saw the heart of Christian doctrine in "brotherly love and unitie."[4] He was

appalled in an equal measure by two offences against Christian
love: by disunity and persecution in religion, and by social
injustice. His remedy for religious disunity consisted, in
addition to complete religious toleration, in a form of worship
reminiscent of a Quaker meeting, without the violent fanaticism
of the early Friends. He implored Cromwell to institute
everywhere "one general Christian assembly or meeting Place."
There the Scriptures would be read at set times, "all sitting
still so long after the reading of the scriptures . . . till anyone
think it fit (in his judicious and humble mind) to propose somewhat for mutual edification, endeavouring withall to make his
discourse short, that another may have his turn likewise."
People would continue to be members of their particular church
or sect, but their common experience and friendly intercourse in
these meetings would result in "a clearing of the misunderstanding" and "a yielding, submissive, condescending love."

The same "love and brotherly sociablenesse" was to be
shown by Christians in their social relations. The title of
Cornelius' second pamphlet was *A Way Propounded to make
the poor of these and other Nations happy*. In it he tried to
distinguish as sharply as possible between the Christian way of
handling these matters and the way of the world. "No pain-
fuller or miserabler thing can be thought on," he wrote, "than
that life which a man lives according to the course of this
world. . . . The world's greatness, and the greatness of
Christians differ as light and darkness." In the world all
greatness lay in "domineering," in different degrees of
"Dignities, States, Frilles and offices." Among Christians,
on the other hand, there should be equality; all Christendom
should be one "great fraternity," and the "means of subsistence
in the world (for necessity and delight) should be common."
A Christian life was also, rightly understood, a natural life;
God, the creator of nature, had "chalked out in nature itself . . .
the amicable and friendly conversations of men." Once again
we meet the classical conception, contained in Stoic philosophy,
of a life *secundum naturam*, a life of moderation in a "society of
mutuall love," without the unnecessary accumulation of

L

wealth and pomp so dear to the men of the world, and without the "painful and laboursome inventions" making life more difficult and causing interminable trouble. These artificial interests, Cornelius believed, had quite obscured the ideas of a good and natural life, but this had not been so "in the primitive times." The call was therefore twofold: back to nature and back to the brotherhood of the early Christians, so as to recover what had been lost.[5]

Cornelius does not seem to have been one of those who were hoping for a large-scale reformation of mankind. Who knows what disappointments he had already experienced? He did not, at any rate, envisage more than the forming of a small model community "in such places as are separate from other men, where we may with less impediment or hindrance, love one another, and mind the wonders of God."[6] We happen to know that in 1662 Cornelius with twenty-four associates borrowed money from the Amsterdam magistrates for the foundation of a colony in America, in which he hoped to realise his principles; and his second English pamphlet contained a similar appeal with the statement that such colonies had been successfully planted in Transylvania, Hungary, and the Palatinate.[7] It was a time when enterprising colonists were wanted in many undeveloped or devastated parts of Europe as well as overseas, and this fact had its effect on social specula- tion. Cornelius' actual plan was not based on complete com- munism but envisaged a separation between the common stock and private goods. All members were to work six hours a day for the common benefit, using the rest of the time "for the refreshing of their bodies, and profitable exercises of the mind," but if they wanted to do additional work for themselves they were at liberty to do so. The profit of the common work was to be used for the common livelihood, and part of the surplus distributed among the members for private disposal. The society was to have its own physicians and surgeons, and experts in mathematics, astronomy, physics, and book-keeping, as well as Latin, Greek, Hebrew, music, and "other usefull things, referring all to a good and spiritual end."[8] The administration of the society was to be on a democratic basis, the necessary officials being elected by universal suffrage, and none of them ruling longer than one year ("least he domineer in his office"[9]). Cornelius regarded these ideas as the solution of both spiritual and material problems. "It becometh us," he wrote, "who hope for the inheritance of our eternal life, in all things to go beyond those that know only this present." This hope of the Beyond, so far from weakening their earthly endeavours, should inspire Christians to order their social affairs in a way which would be worthy of their Master. True rest and perfection could only be attained by building a society of brothers; for Christians, individual salvation and social justice were inseparable.[10]

The Transylvanian and Hungarian communities referred to by Cornelius in support of his appeal were settlements of the Moravian Brethren, whose bishop at that time was Comenius. Cornelius may have heard of them in Holland, but it is also possible that his information came from Samuel Hartlib, Comenius' friend and apostle in England, who in one of his letters quoted a full description of such a colony of the Moravian Brethren from the pen of Comenius' son-in-law. In the same letter he also quoted an enthusiastic recommendation of Peter Cornelius' scheme from John Beale, a scientific writer of note and a very early Fellow of the Royal Society. Beale's remarks are profoundly interesting. "I do extremely indulge," he writes, "the design of beginning the Buildings of Christian Societies in small Models. . . . O that all the religious houses of the Christian world were reformed into true societies, or that our English monasteries could be thus restored! But it seems we men are prompt enough to pull down, and then leave it to God to plant, build, and reform, whilst we talk big of reforming laws, and making whole nations churches and of erecting the Kingdom of Christ all over the world."[11] A Protestant scientist regretting the dissolution of the monasteries: this is certainly worth pondering. The spirit of Little Gidding is again appearing in an unexpected place. And we are reminded by this illuminating statement that all the social endeavours described in this study took place in a country in which the social principles of monasticism were not represented and therefore in danger of falling into oblivion.

Samuel Hartlib[12] has just been mentioned as being in touch with Cornelius; as in many other cases he showed the goodness of his heart in helping this poor foreigner by canvassing for his schemes. This was only one of his innumerable activities which he pursued throughout his life, not sparing money or labour. Son of a merchant of Elbing (Prussia) and an English mother, he was a merchant himself and came to England probably in 1628. From then onwards we find him restlessly engaged in furthering Comenius' educational reform, John Dury's indefatigable endeavours for ecclesiastical peace, various plans for the improvement of husbandry, and many other schemes. In addition he was intensely interested in all scientific matters and was acquainted with several Fellows of the future Royal Society. He was, in fact, one of the *virtuosi*: in the words of John Evelyn, a fellow *virtuoso*, he was "master of innumerable curiosities and very communicative."[13]

It was chiefly Hartlib's belief in science that was underlying his views on social reform. This is most clearly brought out in his short Utopia of 1641, *A Description of the famous Kingdome of Macaria*. In his ideal state there were five executive Councils: for husbandry, fishing, trade by sea, trade by land, and new plantations. The council for husbandry laid down that "if any man holdeth more land than he is able to improve at the utmost, he shall be admonished . . . and if hee doe not amend his Husbandry within a yeares space, there is a penalty set upon him, which is yeerely doubled, till his lands be forfeited."[14] The foremost aim of this *lex agraria* was evidently to achieve the highest possible productive capacity in agriculture by scientific farming. In reforming human society Hartlib mainly relied on spreading the ideas contained in Francis Bacon's *De Augmentis Scientiarum*, and on the use of "the most profitable Inventions . . . unto the benefit of the State." It is also characteristic of him that he seems to have set high hopes, with regard to the cure of poverty, on an elaborate machinery resembling a modern labour exchange.[15] There can be no doubt that Hartlib was a sincere Christian and that he regarded social reform as a precept of Christianity (the relief of poverty was among his strongest concerns), but he arrived at the conclusion so widely held in our own day that science was the safest guide to Utopia. It is not our task in this context to discuss the significance of this attitude. We cannot describe the transition from the enthusiastic hopes of Hartlib and Comenius and their wide circle of friends all over Europe to the results, both spell-casting and disenchanting, of modern science—the transition, we might say, from a certain idea of a Christian Society to the reality of the Royal Society. Here we can only touch on this subject in order to throw into relief the difference between the outlook of this Baconian and the beliefs of the other men who appear in this study.

This difference can be brought before our minds with particular force by considering, in conclusion, a very remarkable writer of the period, the anonymous author of a pamphlet called *Tyranipocrit: Discovered with his wiles, wherewith he vanquisheth.* If this writer was an Englishman (and this is likely, despite the fact that his work purports to be published in Rotterdam), he showed a European consciousness unusual among Englishmen at any time, and unique among his fellow Radicals. His pamphlet was published in 1649, at an important moment in European history. In October 1648 the Peace Conference of Münster and Osnabrück had put an end to the Thirty Years' War, and the future seemed more hopeful. In England the victorious Army had just executed the King and abolished the House of Lords; it seemed that here too the political convulsions had come to an end and some people expected great things from the new rulers. Our author, however, did not share any of these hopes. "Now at this present time," he wrote, "are assembled at Münster the agents of most of our supreame christian Rulers, and what to doe? Or to what end? Not to destroy tyrany . . . but to divide it, and to part the slaves, that every tyrant may abuse his slaves at his owne pleasure." He had nothing better to say of either party in the English Civil War. Charles had been a bad King, but his enemies were bad too. "All of them were Tyrants, and did rob the poor people," and the outcome was "no bettering, but all to establish tyrany in other forms and fashions."[16]

The writer of *Tyranipocrit* did not leave his readers in any doubt about the nature of this tyranny. To him tyranny consisted in the exploitation of the poor by the rich. "Rich and proud tyrants," he maintained, "do rule the christian world," and therefore "men do labour to make themselves rich, that so they may be chosen to be rulers," and, contrary to God's commandment, live "by the sweat of other men's browes." As is evident from the title of his pamphlet he attacked any hypocritical attempts to cover up the naked fact of social tyranny. "I aime at these dubble sinnes," he wrote, "which are esteemed for vertues," for "the devil's kingdome is established through iniquity, and yet it has a show of equity." He was particularly incensed by any attempt to ascribe material prosperity to God's providence—that Puritan attitude which has loomed so large in recent discussions. "The rich artificiall thieves," was his opinion, "do rob the poore, and that under a fained show of justice, and a seeming holinesse, and when they have done it, most impiously they say and affirm that God's providence hath made them rich." Nothing could be further from the truth as proclaimed by Christ who "was poore in worldly wealth, because that is best pleasing unto God. . . . To be rich and pious . . . is impossible."[17]

The evils of tyranny with its supporting hypocrisy could only be avoided by the strictest economic and social equality, and this was, indeed, a precept of Christ. "To give unto every man with discretion so neere as may bee an equall share of earthly goods, is consonant to the law of God and nature, and agreeable to the rule of Christ. . . . In the primitive Church the Christians had their goods in common." "If you should make and maintain an equality of goods and lands, . . . as God and nature would have, as justice and reason doth crave, . . . then mankind might live in love and concord as brethren should doe, . . . then tyranny and oppression would cease and the

TÝRANIPOCRIT,

Diſcovered with his wiles, wherewith he vanquiſheth.

VVritten and printed, to animate better Artiſts to purſue that MONSTER

Aug: 14ᵗʰ

ROTTERDAM,

Printed in the year of our Lord, 1649.

The title-page of *Tyranipocrit*

Kingdome of Christ would flourish." Of course, such a teaching was bound to be ridiculous to the "world," but God had given to every man a "sparke of his owne essence" and so made possible man's complete reformation. "God so formed man," wrote this Christian humanist, "that hee is capable of divine wisdom, not by compulsion but by reason; not by force, but by free-will." Because of God's grace, all the means of our individual and social salvation were in our hands and hearts; we had only to make use of them.[18]

From this point of view, a number of other social phenomena came in for bitter criticism. War, for example, was nothing else but the killing of one tyrant's slaves by the slaves of his neighbour tyrant; it was always a case of one innocent killing another.[19] An interesting, and at that time unusual, attack was directed against the growing colonial trade. "Our merchants, they travel by Sea and Land, to make Christian proselites, chiefly our Indian merchants; but consider their practices, and the profite that wee have by their double dealing, first in robbing of the poore Indians of that which God and nature hath given them, and then in bringing of it home to us, that wee thereby may the better set forth and show the pride of our hearts, in decking of our proud carcases and feeding of our greedy gutts with superfluous, unnecessary curiosities." And here we also hear a protest, for a long time to come uncomfortably rare among Europeans, against colonial slavery: "Although their dealings with the Indians goods bee bad, yet they deale worser with their persons; for they either kill them, which is bad, or make them their slaves, which is worse."[20]

Whoever this enemy of tyranny and hypocrisy may have been, he had an exceptionally independent mind and a remarkable power of pungent and vivid expression. At the time of writing, he tells us, he was separated from his books, but we can imagine him sitting in his library and looking at the turbulent world outside with his eyes sharpened by the experience of a lifetime, and his mind illumined by the Christian message. He belonged to those who weighed their society in the scales of Christ and found it wanting.

NOTES TO CHAPTER NINE

1 *Original Letters . . . Addressed to Oliver Cromwell . . .*, ed. by John Nickalls (1743), pp. 99, 102. The letter is dated 4th Aug. 1653.

2 His full name, in the contemporary spelling, seems to have been Pieter Cornelisz Plockboy van Ziercksee: cf. Laspeyres, *Geschichte der volkswirthschaftlichen Anschauungen der Niederländer* (1863), p. 105.

3 His first letter to Cromwell is dated 24th June 1658 (*Somers Tracts*, vi 487–97).

4 *Somers Tracts*, vi, 471.

5 Cornelius, *A Way Propounded*, pp. 3, 24, 25, 29, 31, 32.

6 Cornelius, ibid., p. 31.

7 Laspeyres, op. cit., p. 105; Cornelius, op. cit., Appendix.

8 Cornelius, op. cit., pp. 4, 6.

9 Cornelius, ibid., p. 8. Cornelius' community in New Netherland was destroyed by English colonists in 1664. Cornelius himself was seen in Germantown, Pennsylvania, in 1694—an old, blind beggar. (Bernstein, *Sozialismus und Demokratic in der grossen Englischen Revolution*, 2. Auflage, 1908, p. 290.)

10 Cornelius, ibid., pp. 33, 34.

11 *The Diary and Correspondence of Dr. John Worthington*, ed. James Crossley, Chetham Society, 1847, i, 158.

12 On Hartlib, cf. Friedrich Althaus, *Samuel Hartlib, ein deutsch-englisches Charakterbild* (*Historisches Taschenbuch* (1884)); G. H. Turnbull, *Samuel Hartlib* (1920).

13 *Evelyn's Diary*, ed. Bray, i, 310.

14 Hartlib, *Macaria*, p. 4.

15 Hartlib, *A brief Discourse Concerning the Accomplishment of our Reformation* (1647), p. 47, *passim*.

16 *Tyranipocrit*, pp. 19, 54, 35. D. W. Petegorsky is the only writer, as far as I know, who has mentioned this pamphlet (*Left-Wing Democracy in the English Civil War*, pp. 29, 232–3), but no reader of his carefully pruned extracts could gather that its author was inspired by Christian spiritualism.

17 *Tyranipocrit*, pp. 3, 4, 16, 17, 33.

18 Ibid., pp. 8, 19, 33.

19 Ibid., p. 24.

20 Ibid., p. 23.

CHAPTER TEN

THE BROTHERHOOD OF MAN

WE have listened carefully to the words of these men. We have deliberately refrained from interrupting them too often and from asking them questions which they could not understand. Several times we may have wished that they had been more explicit and informative: nothing short of resurrection could entirely satisfy us. But we may feel that by now we know something about their minds and characters. As always, we are impressed by the variety of human life. We have met the excitable and the even-tempered, the self-righteous and the humble, the humorous and the all-too-serious, those who had an axe to grind and those who were unselfish. Some were very poor, others lived in moderate well-being; some had read widely, others despised all books; some were inclined to ecstasy and fanaticism, others managed to keep a cool head. But despite these differences there was much they had in common. Almost all of them, true children of an Age of Faith, were strongly and deeply influenced by the religious currents of their time. The English nation was about to become "the People of one Book," and it was, above all, the Bible that provided these men with constant material for their thought. The Bible is, of course, really more than one book. It has rightly been described as a library of religious books, and these books contain many different and, as some people think, conflicting things. Now it is not easy to generalise about the attitude of these men to the various parts of the Bible; here too there was some diversity. Not all of them, certainly, were Antinomians. Some of them, it is true, prized the Gospels above everything else, perhaps together with the First Epistle of John, but others drew constant inspiration from certain parts of the Old Testament, especially from some of the prophetic writings. While some based all their views on Christian love, others relied also on the firm conceptions of social justice contained in the Old Testament, applying to Christians what the prophets had demanded of the Jewish people.

We have found that underlying much of their thought on social matters was the desire for equality. There can be no doubt that a certain conception of equality is inherent in Christianity. All men are children of the same Father, and salvation through Christ is offered to all, including harlots and publicans. "There is neither Jew nor Greek, there is neither bond nor free, there is neither male nor female: for ye are all one in Christ Jesus" (Gal. iii, 28). This in itself does not amount to a programme of social reform; it simply means that to a Christian all inequalities (some of which are clearly unalterable) are outweighed by the equality in Christ.[1] The central and dominant tradition of Christianity has always accepted social as well as natural inequality, but it has demanded the permeation of all social relationships by the Christian spirit. In course of time, the "Christian master" and the "Christian servant" became concepts of thought and recognisable moral images; so did the "Christian king" and the "Christian knight." (In the Middle Ages, it should be noted, no concept of the "Christian rich man" was developed.) But in addition to this central tradition, there was also a Christian undercurrent (its origins do not concern us here) which attempted to translate the idea of Christian equality into social reforms. Some institutions of this world, notably magistracy and private property, were often held to be incompatible with Christianity. Christians, it was said, were not to have dominion one over another, and had not the Apostles shared all their goods among themselves? It was also stressed again and again that at the time of Adam and Eve there had been no gentlemen (here, pictures of the state of nature, older than Christianity, were inextricably combined with Christian ideas). It is likely that these convictions had an underground existence throughout

the Middle Ages and beyond. We get occasional glimpses of
them in such sectarian movements as the Waldenses, the
Fraticelli, and the radical Hussites, and during the upheaval
caused by the Lutheran Reformation in Germany we come
across all the radical tendencies displayed in England over a
century later: in Hipler's democratic reforms, in the Twelve
Articles of the Peasants, in the communist millennia of Thomas
Münzer and the Anabaptists, and in the Mennonites' pacifism.
The upheaval caused by the Puritan Revolution set free very
similar forces.

The main current of Puritanism, however, was not favourable
to Christian equality. This has been attributed to the doctrine
of predestination with its sharp and unbridgeable division
between the elect and the damned. But this doctrine in itself
is quite compatible, as in Lilburne's case, with a certain belief
in social equality, for who knows, before Judgment Day, who
will be among the elect? It is only when worldly success is
regarded as a mark of spiritual election that social inequality
receives its religious justification.

How this occurred within Puritanism has often been described,
and does not need to be repeated here; how economic activities
in particular, hitherto seldom looked at without grave suspicion,
were surrounded with a halo; and how a large section of social
morality underwent a process of revaluation. The undercurrent of Puritanism described in this study represented a
determined protest against this development. Its members,
as we have repeatedly pointed out, were unmistakable Puritans,
but they also showed important characteristics of their own.
Their sense of community was, on the whole, more acute than
their individualism; their beliefs made them more aware of the
tension between Judaeo-Christian ethics and the social institutions of the world, and so they were led to suspect many
features of social, economic and political life which most of their
contemporaries were prepared to accept.

A word should be said here about the most famous of these
contemporaries, Oliver Cromwell. His name has frequently
been mentioned in these pages. He was, for a time at least, a

friend of Lilburne's; acquainted with Walwyn; impressed by Saltmarsh; well disposed towards Fox; prepared to have a discussion with Rogers; and accessible to Chidley and Cornelius. He was evidently not quite without sympathy for the aims of these men. At Putney, during the debate about the Agreement of the People, he said: "I cannot see but that we all speak to the same end. . . . The end is to deliver this nation from oppression and slavery, to accomplish that work that God hath carried us on in, to establish our hopes of an end of justice and righteousness in it."[2] It is, however, very difficult to know what precisely he meant by such words as "oppression" and "justice." Cromwell's ideas, shaped by the events more than shaping them, were at no time of his life particularly clear. The most pressing social problems of his day did engage his attention at various stages of his career, but the legislation passed during the period of his leadership did very little to bring them nearer to solution or to check the acquisitive tendencies of the possessing classes. Moreover, Cromwell was no friend of social equality. In the opening speech to the first Parliament of the Protectorate he proclaimed his intention to uphold the traditional social distinctions: "A nobleman, a gentleman, a yeoman: that is a good interest of the Nation, and a great one." But he does not seem to have been aware that the very foundations of the old social order were threatened.

The protest of the Puritan Radicals occurred at a time of a profound social crisis, and in a country which, of all European countries, had probably advanced furthest on the road to modern society, with its expanding trade and industry, complex social relationships, and widening class-divisions. It was a society in which, owing to its impersonal structure, it became increasingly difficult to be guided by personal social ethics. Things were, so to speak, happening behind one's back; enmeshed in the network of the stock exchange or the world-market, one found it hard to apply the old precepts. R. H. Tawney has reproached the Church for not having given new answers to these new questions and for having confined herself to a protest the very terms of which were bound to make it appear vague. "Granted," he writes, "that I should love my neighbour as myself, the questions which, under modern conditions of large-scale organization, remain for solution are, Who precisely *is* my neighbour? and, How exactly am I to make my love for him effective in practice? To these questions the conventional religious teaching supplied no answer, for it had not even realised that they could be put."[3] Something like this could be said about the Puritan Radicals too. Their protest was in some respects vague (their failure to recognise the importance of the copyholders' security of tenure is perhaps a case in point). They too were not able to understand the full complexity of the new problems, and some of the reforms they suggested were impracticable. But, on the other hand, there were some among them who showed a clear grasp of social realities and a shrewd estimation of contemporary affairs. Some of their reforming proposals, especially concerning tithes, poor relief, and the franchise, could have easily been carried out. And a man like the author of *Tyranipocrit* knew quite well that, under modern conditions, the natives of India were included among his neighbours.

The Puritan Radicals were not able to arrest the social transformation then in progress. The Levellers were soon almost completely forgotten, and there is a remarkable absence of social criticism in England during the later seventeenth century and almost the whole of the eighteenth. It might seem that the Puritan Radicals were, as history mercilessly calls it, a failure. But this would be saying too much. Something of their spirit lived on in the surviving sectarian bodies. Among the Puritan sectarians, especially among the Quakers, there were to be found again and again men of sturdy independence and fearless character who would denounce social evils and conduct movements for social reform. The liberal and radical movements of the nineteenth century were closely bound up with the nonconformist sects, and it is equally true that some of the early history of the Labour movement took place in chapels and church halls and was shaped by men who had received their schooling in their local religious organisations.

In this way England was saved from the fateful separation, so marked on the Continent, of religion and social reform. This spirit became part of the common English heritage, and therefore it could be alive in Christian men and women both within and beyond the circle of nonconformity: in Woolman and Wilberforce, Howard and Fry, Shaftesbury and Dickens, Cobbett and Carlyle, Ruskin and Kingsley, Gore and Temple, Gill and Chesterton, and many others without a name.

Nevertheless, despite these survivals, it remains true that the growth of modern society, with its specifically modern outlook, proved irresistible. We have mentioned above the direct effect of Puritanism on the sanctification of the business virtues, but it must be added that the next step—the thoroughly modern conviction that religion is one thing and business quite another —was reached surprisingly quickly. Religion ceased to be all-embracing; secular affairs, it was increasingly believed, could well look after themselves. Now this process of secularisation was in many ways resisted by the Puritan Radicals, yet they themselves were not able to escape its immensely powerful influence, and both directly and indirectly they had a share in it too. It has been suggested by A. S. P. Woodhouse, in a most illuminating essay, that the Protestant separation of Nature and Grace had a secularising effect, especially among some of the extreme sectarians. According to them, the Holy Community of believers was under the exclusive rule of Grace, which was utterly different from the rule imposed on those who remained outside. A church had to legislate for the just and the unjust; a sect could not and would not. Thus, by shutting the gates of Grace on the many who were not chosen, these sectarians made room for purely secular influences outside the realm of Grace. This line of thought, in Woodhouse's words, "which issues in a purely spiritual view of the church issues just as certainly in a purely secular view of the state."[4] This "principle of segregation" was not at work in all the Puritan Radicals, not even in all the Levellers, but it does, for example, apply to Lilburne: we have noted his peculiar combination of a very strong sectarianism with a strikingly secular outlook in politics.[5]

Recalling what we found in an earlier chapter, we can say that another tendency towards secularisation, though a more indirect one, was bound up with the "religion of the Spirit." Sectarianism had undermined the traditional conception of a church, but the spiritual religion endangered the existence of church and sect alike, indeed of any religious body. Its anticlericalism and dogmatic antidogmatism contributed in the long run to making religion an exclusively private affair, and its insistence on spiritual fulfilment in this life combined with other influences in weakening the hold of transcendental ideas over men's minds. This type of religion, it should also be borne in mind, is notoriously liable to be rather vague, and this vagueness was enhanced by that liking for symbolism which we have noticed on several occasions. Symbolism, to be sure, was a widespread mental habit in the seventeenth century: it was one of the attempts to find out the innermost truth about the universe and so to achieve the synthesis of knowledge and faith. To Sir Thomas Browne, the book of Nature was full of profound symbols initiating him into the mysteries of God and His creation. But this temper did not survive the triumph of modern science; in a more "enlightened" climate of opinion symbolism was doomed either to wither away or to lose itself in ever more subjective and abstruse forms, far away from the central stream of speculation. The reception of Jakob Böhme's system marks the beginning of a development which was to lead to Swedenborg and Blake, and to the numerous theosophical groups of a later date. It is indeed possible to regard everything as a parable, but in the end there were too many private systems of parables, and meanwhile the world proceeded on its confident course without any parables at all.

A similar effect resulted from the attacks made by some of the Puritan Radicals on the traditional culture of Church and University. By cutting themselves off from this rich heritage of contemplation and wisdom they helped to destroy the precarious balance of their civilisation and laid it open to the onslaught of a narrowly scientific and utilitarian conception of life. Some of their criticisms of contemporary scholarship were justified, but they did not discriminate between the real culprits and men like Hales or Selden. This attitude could easily combine with the contempt spread by the "New Philosophy" for the learning of the "Schools."

Considerations such as these help us to understand the sudden transition, after 1660, from an Age of Faith to the Age of Reason. But if there are affinities between the later view of life and that of the Puritan Radicals, the differences are much greater. To stress this is particularly necessary because, as we have seen above, some of the Puritan Radicals are often described as present-day democrats, communists, or rationalists, born before their time. Such descriptions are bound to ignore some very important facts. Before 1660, and in the social strata where radicalism was at home, religion was still the shaping and inspiring force, and religion was still, in spite of changes and signs of decay, an all-embracing system of beliefs and assumptions with deep and complex roots in the past. One could indicate the historical position of the Puritan Radicals by saying that in their criticism of society they had much more in common with William Langland than with Thomas Paine or Karl Marx. In *Piers Plowman* we find the vision of Lady Meed, symbolising "a society intoxicated by the power of wealth and governed by purely economic motives."[6] Against this is set the vision of Jesus Christ who is seen in the guise of a simple peasant, of Piers the Plowman himself:

And in the apparel of a poor man . and a pilgrim's likeness
Many times God has been met . among needy people.

And Christ is also the foundation and guarantee of human brotherhood:

For all we are Christ's creatures . and of his coffers rich,
And brethren as of one blood . as well beggars as earls,
For on Calvary of Christ's blood . Christendom gan spring,
And blood brethren we became there . of one body won.

The corresponding later assumptions are profoundly different. Democracy largely based on the ideas of 1789 or on utilitarian

M

ethics; communism supported by dialectical materialism; and agnostic rationalism—these are products, for good or ill, of the eighteenth and nineteenth centuries. Its adherents should not try, like some *nouveaux riches*, to establish a spurious pedigree.

But there is more to it than that. In order to bring out the full significance of the cleavage between seventeenth-century radicalism and its later counterparts it will be necessary to investigate rather more closely the process of secularisation. It is not sufficient to describe it merely in terms of the growing interest in secular matters and the corresponding decline of transcendental ideas. It also resulted in the loss of a balanced and comprehensive system of thought, derived from the old-established union of Christian and classical sources. By "system of thought" more is meant than a conscious structure of philosophy and theology, though that had been created too. These ideas, in one form or another, had penetrated to people who had never heard of philosophy; without them nothing could be thought at all; they had shaped the very assumptions which, in any given age, are taken for granted without any further enquiry. The effects of these beliefs were so far-reaching that they constitute, in a sense, the history of the European mind between antiquity and modern times. Here we shall have to be content with concentrating on one aspect of particular relevance to this study.

In that system of thought secular things were never regarded quite without suspicion. Their claims to be ends in themselves, or even goods in themselves, were not accepted, their ultimate justification was held to lie outside them. The workings of state, law, or trade, for example, were all judged by standards which could not be deduced from politics, jurisprudence, or economics alone. Directed by these standards, man, a rational being, was capable of an ordered and significant life on earth in various social communities, and of eternal life hereafter in the communion of the Saints. On the other hand, owing to the Fall, he was also capable of playing "such fantastic tricks before high heaven as make the angels weep"; the world was under a curse and in need of redeeming Grace from above. Thus a dual attitude to the world, both favourable and unfavourable, was possible and indeed necessary. One could create cultural values of all kinds, and yet be aware of the inescapable limitation of all human endeavour—an awareness which may be a prerequisite of civilised life. (It was this complex awareness, as we have seen, that produced the judgments of such men as Hales and Chillingworth.) Moreover, Christianity does not allow men either to escape the responsibility for their shortcomings or to be overwhelmed by them. A Christian civilisation requires a simultaneous existence on two levels: on the level of the world, and on the level of the Christian teaching which corrects, transforms, and transfigures the world. The resulting fruitful tension has been admirably described by Mr. Middleton Murry, who speaks of the necessity to realise that the Kingdom of God on earth *cannot* be established, and that the Kingdom of God on earth *must* be established.[7]

Such a dual attitude is bound to disappear in the fully secularised world of our time. The same social institutions which were formerly regarded as either necessary or unnecessary evils are now accepted as inherently harmless or good, sometimes even as ends in themselves. There is, of course, a good deal of social criticism directed against what are felt to be social abuses, but increasing trust is placed in political, economic, and, latterly, educational reforms, which, it is supposed, will put an end to these abuses. To many, the solution of all problems lies in the abolition of private property and the unlimited extension of state ownership, but they do not seriously question the institution of the modern state itself. Again, inequality of wealth is being attacked, but wealth as such is no longer suspected. Modern socialists are committed to a programme of making everybody as wealthy as the technique of production will allow, whereas the older radicals were aware of the moral danger inherent in excessive possessions. The author of *Tyranipocrit*, for instance, was stating a representative opinion when he saw the defect of his society "not so much, in that some men are too poore, as . . . in that

M*

some are too rich" (p. 38). Seen from this point of view, it appears that present-day Radicals are not, in fact, truly radical: having neglected the roots of man and the world, they cannot go to the roots of evil. Their earlier counterparts knew certainly less about economics and sociology, but they had a deeper insight into the human situation. Our radical contemporaries should not be given the credit, as they often are, for being realists. It is unrealistic to produce reform plans which are based on a false conception of man.

The growing uncertainty about the nature of man is, indeed, an important feature of the secularising process. It would be a mistake to suppose that the central place, formerly held by God, was afterwards taken by man. The central place of God was not taken by anyone, it remained empty:

> Things fall apart, the centre cannot hold,
> Mere anarchy is loosed upon the world.
>
> (W. B. Yeats)

The sphere of human activities did not emancipate itself as a whole, but one department after another issued special Declarations of Independence. First politics, then science, and still later economics: they all proclaimed the autonomy of their respective realms, complete independence from any laws but their own. Transcendental standards, to be sure, were thus everywhere excluded and man was made the measure of all things, but now there was no picture of man which could count on general acceptance. One could take one's choice from the Political Man, the Scientific Man, the Economic Man, and a number of others as well: all of them about as similar to a real man as a scarecrow. Matters were made worse by repeated attempts to use these one-sided conceptions as a basis for a comprehensive philosophy; the loss of the old balance gave rise to dictatorial desires of the newly emancipated powers. With religion and ethics out of the way, politics proceeded to develop the doctrine of the totalitarian State; economics claimed to have found the sole clue to the history and future of mankind; and science felt confident of being able to sustain alone the whole fabric of human society. The penalties for all these fundamental mistakes are high.

It was the older conception of man that was underlying the Puritan Radical's idea of equality. Most of them thought of equality in terms of human brotherhood, and it is well worth examining what this means.

First of all, many of them, being members of large families, must have had an intimate experience of living with brothers and sisters. In a family there are both equality and inequality. The members are of different ages, of different sexes, of different abilities, of different temperaments. But they belong to the same family, and this equality outweighs their differences. In a small community where all members know each other personally a similar feeling can easily grow up. This is not to suggest that such harmony did, in fact, often exist, only that aiming at it was a commonly acknowledged task. For, secondly, this family feeling was powerfully enforced by the Christian beliefs in the Fatherhood of God, the Sonship of Christ, and the brotherhood of man. In the larger family, as in the smaller, equality was inseparably bound up with love—the love that holds all things together, "l'amor che muove il sol e l'altre stelle." And the love of God was inseparable from the love of one's neighbour: it was man's likeness to God that made him lovable, and "he that loveth not his brother whom he hath seen, how can he love God whom he hath not seen?" (1 John iv, 20).

The reality of such a brotherhood is not primarily dependent on the existence of any specific social institution, but on the spirit pervading society as a whole. It is, however, possible to regard certain institutions as impermeable to the Christian spirit, and on this point the Puritan Radicals were not unanimous. A few of them, supported by a trend within Christianity and by Stoic thought, believed private property to be such an insuperable obstacle. But we can easily understand why this was then by no means the paramount issue that it has become in recent times. Most of these men, thinking in terms of the small freeholder, the artisan, and the shopkeeper, did not find their picture of a society of brothers to be incompatible with moderate private property.

A glance at the prevailing contemporary idea of equality, mainly derived from the *égalité* of the French Revolution, will, once again, reveal a deep gulf. It is significant that of the three slogans of the French Revolution—*liberté*, *égalité*, *fraternité*—the first two have been immensely powerful, while the third has only played a shadowy part. The very fact that fraternity (whatever it may have meant) was separated from equality indicates an important development: if there was to be a feeling of brotherliness at all, it had to be specially evoked; a fraternal bond was no longer implied in the idea of equality.

Here we are faced again with the secularised conception of man, with all its shortcomings. The living person with its manifold social and metaphysical bonds has disappeared, and instead we have to deal with variously conceived abstract entities which have lost so many distinguishing features that their equality, for what it is worth, can easily be asserted. This way of thinking has undermined all the traditional social relationships except one: that of the State, for it is to the State that the most powerful trend of modern thought assigns the task of establishing the desired equality. Thus *égalité* can easily lead to the totalitarian State, which is only capable of a mock-equality of serfdom, however loudly it may claim to fulfil the demands of social justice or to realise the brotherhood of man.

For a Christian there can be no doubt about the remedy. He is aware of the essentially religious nature of society and the essentially social nature of his religion. He too is committed to a certain kind of secularisation: it is his perennial task to Christianise the world, to permeate ever more secular departments with the Christian spirit, to realise on this earth the community of brothers in Christ. He hopes and works for a revival of those transcendental standards which alone, he believes, can reawaken our consciousness and our conscience. He firmly holds that mankind without God cannot retain even its human level and must fall into inhumanity, because the picture of man derives its brightness from being an image of God. And he is convinced that there will be no brotherhood among men who have forgotten their common Father.

NOTES TO CHAPTER TEN

[1] I am following A. D. (now Lord) Lindsay's interpretation of Christian equality in *The Modern Democratic State* (1943), vol. i.

[2] Woodhouse, *Puritanism and Liberty*, p. 104.

[3] Tawney, *Religion and the Rise of Capitalism*, p. 184.

[4] Woodhouse, op. cit., Introduction, p. 59.

[5] Woodhouse also suggests that it was the Antinomianism of the Levellers which, in view of the reticence of the Gospels in political matters, made them rely on secular sources (op. cit., Introduction, p. 87), but some of the available evidence conflicts with this view. Lilburne was not an Antinomian, and Walwyn, who was one, based all his judgments, including those on political matters, on his interpretation of the New Testament.

[6] C. Dawson, *Medieval Religion*, p. 172. The quotations from Langland are taken from the same book; the translation is C. Dawson's.

[7] John Middleton Murry, *Heaven and Earth* (1938), p. 354.

APPENDIX A

RICHARD OVERTON—AN EARLY MATERIALIST?

IN 1644 a book was published called *Man's Mortallitie Or A Treatise Wherein 'tis proved . . . that Man . . . is a Compound wholy mortall, contrary to that common distinction of Soule and Body.* Though the author is mentioned only by his initials "R. O.," the authorship of Richard Overton, the Leveller, is generally accepted. This book was judged important enough to be condemned by Parliament, together with Milton's tract on divorce, and was reprinted, with additions, in 1655 and again in 1674.

Overton argued his case on two levels, "Theologically and Phylosophically," and displayed a certain amount of learning, though this was of a kind that could easily be obtained from popular compilations (certain celebrities, such as Copernicus, Tycho Brahe and Cornelius Agrippa, were obviously quoted to impress the simple reader). A contemporary opponent noticed with indignation Overton's faulty Latin and his constant references to "Nigromancy" instead of "Necromancy."[1] The fortuitous character of Overton's learning is further suggested by the fact that the well-known Aristotelian conception of the soul seems to have been known to him through Nemesius (who had been translated in 1636 by George Wither) and, surprisingly, through the great French surgeon and medical writer Ambroise Paré. Of Descartes' views on the relations of body and soul laid down in *Discours de la Méthode* (1637) and *Meditationes de Prima Philosophia* (1641) Overton knew nothing at all; in all probability he would not have been able to read these books.

Basing his philosophical deliberations on an Aristotelian definition of the soul ("all the internall and externall Faculties of man joyntly considered"), he had no difficulty in proving that a faculty cannot exist without its subject: "accidens non est nisi in subjecto," and—again in the Aristotelian manner—that form cannot exist without matter or matter without form, for "their Being is in this Union, and their Union is in this

168

Being" (pp. 11, 16, 13). If, then, Adam, who had at first been wholly immortal, was by God's decree to be "mortallised by Transgression," all of him, including his soul which could not be separated from the rest, "was lyable to Death by Sinne" (p. 12).

Theological arguments led Overton to the same conclusion. After the Fall, man's soul could be immortal only if it were created afresh at each new birth "by the supernaturall and extraordinairie assistance of God," for it was man's curse that what "proceedeth from Man simply by the course of nature . . . must first tast of mortallity." But, he continued, "it is granted that the body considered meerly sensitive cannot sinne," and that in sinning "the body is but an instrument . . . to the Soul." If, then, the soul were especially created by God, He would be "the Author of all sinne." Therefore the soul cannot be in a different position from the body: "nothing of man can be immortall, but what first hath seen corruption" (pp. 41, 40, 44, 47).

It is not our task to assess the philosophical or theological value of these statements, though we may be permitted to say that they seem to be attempts to deal with genuine problems. We must, however, try to appreciate their contemporary background. The religious fanatic Edward Wightman, who was burned at the stake in 1612, included among his beliefs that both body and soul were asleep after death.[2] A refutation of this doctrine was published in 1611; the author probably referred to Wightman when he wrote that some "Anabaptists" had lately fallen into that error.[3] But this belief was not confined to obscure sectaries: such eminent and learned men as Thomas Browne and Milton held this "mortalist heresy" at one time or another.[4] According to Ephraim Pagitt's *Heresiography* a new sect of "Soul-sleepers" arose round the author of *Man's Mortallitie*,[5] and Edwards' *Gangraena* contains a vivid description of a "Disputation . . . about the Immortality of the Soule by some Anabaptists" in 1646, at which Overton was present. After the first two disputants had spent four or five hours in fruitless discourse, two others got up—"Mellish a Cobler, and Lawson a Schoolmaster, both Anabaptists. . . . Lawson calls to Mellish and saith to him, Brother Mellish, speak either Categorically or Hypothetically, Mellish answered Lawson, that he spake now to him in an unknown tongue, and praied him to explain himself; Lawson told Mellish that he was not fit to to dispute if he knew not the meaning of these words."[6]

This disputation has an undeniable family likeness to the artisans' scenes in *A Midsummer Night's Dream*, but it is clear that these simple people regarded this question as relevant to their quest for religious truth.

Overton must have shared this feeling, and we can even surmise his main aims in writing his book. To him, the conception of the soul which he opposed was the basis of the belief in "Purgatorie, Limbo Patrum, Infantum, Prayers unto dead Saints, to the Virgin Mary, and a World of such like fancies." Apart from this anticatholic tendency, the message of his work was to be a call to humility in view of "Man's Foundation" being "wholy in the Dust"; finding that he has not even an immortal soul, man will be all the more "provoaked . . . to cast himselfe wholy on Jesus Christ" (pp. 55–7). Thomas Browne, incidentally, seems to have been prompted by similar considerations: "Surely," he wrote, "it is but the merits of our unworthy Natures, if we sleep in darkness until the last Alarum."[7] That "last Alarum," it should not be overlooked, was unquestioningly accepted by Overton: the ultimate resurrection was "the beginning of our immortality" when the righteous would appear in glory with Christ. He maintained, indeed, that the value of the resurrection might be impaired by the belief that only man's lesser part, his body, had been made mortal by the Fall, while the soul had continued to be immortal (title-page, pp. 57, 3).

It would, then, be difficult to agree with A. S. P. Woodhouse that Overton "advances a materialistic view of man and the world," or to regard him, with other historians, as a predecessor of modern scientific materialism.[8] Overton never asserted either that the soul does not exist or that it consists of matter; he merely argued, on the grounds set out above, that it could not exist by itself and so had to share with the body the same process of death and resurrection. Woodhouse attempts to strengthen his view of Overton as belonging "to no religious tradition" by stating that he "studiously ignores the Fall."[9] But we have seen that this is not the case at all; the whole line of thought in *Man's Mortallitie* does, indeed, presuppose the Fall. Overton did, in fact, belong to a religious tradition, and to one which would hardly have allowed him to ignore the Fall: he was a Baptist. When he joined that sect in Holland, he wrote a Baptist declaration of faith,[10] and he seems to have remained a Baptist at least up to 1649, when we begin to lose sight of his religious development. During his imprisonment in that year he complained bitterly of being persecuted by his "very brethren the Church-men,"[11] but not even that could make him renounce his membership of his congregation, because he knew "its institution to be holy and good."[12] There is no reason to assume that he ever abandoned his belief in the Christian dogmas to which he proclaimed allegiance in his declaration of faith. Seen from the point of view of the predominant Christian tradition, his "Soul-sleeping" is a heresy, but it is not a premature advance into modern philosophy.

NOTES TO APPENDIX A

[1] Anon., *The Prerogative of Man* (1645).

[2] Champlin Burrage, *Early English Dissenters*, i, 219.

[3] John Jackson, *The Soul is Immortall*, 1611, ff. A.2, A.3.

[4] Thomas Browne, *Religio Medici* (Everyman's edition), p. 8; Milton, *Christian Doctrine*, I, xiii (cf. *Paradise Lost*, x, 789).

[5] Ephraim Pagitt, *Heresiography*, 3rd ed. (1647), p. 148.

[6] Thomas Edwards, *Gangraena*, ii, 17.

[7] Thomas Browne, loc. cit.

[8] Woodhouse, *Puritanism and Liberty*, Introduction, p. 55; Petegorsky, *Left-Wing Democracy in the English Civil War*, pp. 72-3; E. Bernstein, *Cromwell and Communism* (1930), p. 90; G. Lenz, *Demokratie und Diktatur in der Englischen Revolution* (*Historische Zeitschrift*, Beiheft 28), pp. 59-60.

[9] Woodhouse, op. cit., pp. 55, 90.

[10] Printed in full in B. Evans, *The Early English Baptists* (1862), pp. 254-6.

[11] This obviously refers to the Baptist attack against the imprisoned Leveller leaders in *Walwins Wiles* by W. Kiffin and others.

[12] Richard Overton, *Overton's Defyance of the Act* (1649), p. 4.

APPENDIX B

JOHN JUBBES' AGREEMENT OF THE PEOPLE

In December 1648 a pamphlet was published in London, called *Severall Proposals for Peace and Freedom, by an Agreement of the People, Offered unto Commissary General Ireton for the Convenience of the Army by the Approbation and Consent of many worthy Persons of the Common Counsel and others of the City of London . . . To be Agreed unto, and Inscribed by all the Inhabitants of England and Wales.* It contained proposals for a constitutional settlement and various other reforms, showing obvious traces of the Leveller Agreement of the People of 1647. Its most important provisions were these: "That the People do of course choose themselves a Parliament once every two years, after the most free and uncontrolable manner. . . . That the People being at this time very unequally distributed for electing their Representatives, shall be more indifferently proportioned . . .; and that not only every Free-holder, but Copy-holder also that is worth forty shillings per annum, and every other person that is worth 50 L. personall estate, may have Voyces in the Elections thereof. . . . If the King shall Assent unto this Agreement, that then He may be Proclaimed and Crowned King again. And who . . . may in a Parliamentary way have as great an Annual Revenue conferred upon him, as (one year with another of his Reign) was yet ever brought into the Exchequer, notwithstanding those vast illegal sums thereof, raised by the multitude of Monopolies, and destroying usurping Projects, Except what shall be defrayed for such Charges as henceforth shall be thought fit to be defrayed by the Parliament, which formerly was done by the King. . . . That if any King of England shall hereafter challenge to himself a Negative Voyce, to the Determinations of the Representative in Parliament . . . [he] may be deposed by the same Parliament."[1]

This document, which has been referred to as the Third Agreement of the People,[2] is more moderate, on the whole, than the Levellers' Agreement. It is probable that its supporters were connected with the sectarian and democratic agitation in the City of London, and one might have expected to find its author in those circles. This, however, is not the case. The author was almost certainly John Jubbes, who was a member of the Parliamentarian Army from 1643 to 1648, and rose to be Lieutenant-Colonel in Colonel Hewson's regiment.

A pamphlet called *An Apology . . . by Lieut.-Col. John Jubbes Touching His Proceeding in a Paper (called Proposals for Peace and Freedom . . .)*, contains as an appendix an almost literal, if slightly rearranged, version of the Third Agreement of the People, the substance of which John Jubbes claims to have drawn up.[3] This statement is supported by internal evidence, such as the similarity of the style of both pamphlets (Jubbes' penmanship was, to put it mildly, confused and clumsy), and the frequent reiteration of certain favourite topics, e.g. the settlement of Ireland. He goes on to say that he showed the paper to many officers, including Fairfax, Rainborough and Harrison (a representative collection!); they all approved of it except, not surprisingly, Ireton: "with him it stuck and went no further." When the document was presented to Ireton by some citizens after the army had entered London (2nd December 1648), "he was pleased to cause answer to be returned that it was then too late" (which explains a little the ineffectiveness of this Agreement).

I have not been able to discover anything about Jubbes' life outside the Army. It is possible that he belonged to a family of Norfolk landowners,[4] but there is nothing to support this, except the unusual name. His political activity can be traced back to the statement of the grievances of Hewson's regiment (13th May 1647), which was signed by Jubbes, Axtell and two agitators, and put forward "not only the common desires of the privates as soldiers, but certain political demands; one was that the freemen of England were liable to arbitrary imprisonment, another that the laws of the land were in an unknown tongue."[5]

Jubbes had indeed, like so many others, joined the Parliamentary army because he "had been long deeply sensible of the many greevous Incroachments and Usurpations exercised over the People of this Nation"; he was loud in his condemnation of the "mercinary beast and murtherer."[6] He also took part in the agitation for the Levellers' Agreement of the People in November 1647.[7]

On 1st November 1647, during the Putney debates, he advanced, for the first time, his scheme for the reinstatement of the King, after a purge of the House of Commons, expressing anxiety lest there be another Civil War and further effusion of blood.[8] But his hopes for a peaceful settlement were diminished by the suppression of the Army Levellers, that "sad thing," after which "Mr. Saltmarsh [left] his life." He was obviously impressed by Saltmarsh, whose "love to righteousness" he praised. When he finally "discovered Resolutions to grounds and foundations of a lasting War" he laid down his sword.[9]

It is evident from Jubbes' account that religious scruples played a great part in making him leave the Army. "Truly," he said, "I did not fight for the fame of Alexander but Christ," and when he considered laying down his commission, he "was forc'd to inquire again what God was."[10] And this is what he found: "By my observations of the orderly motion of the glorious Bodies of the Sun, Moon, Earth and Stars, [I] do know, that something put (and keeps) them in order. . . . And as this God did, so he doth create all things good and nothing evill. . . . Man is endued . . . with a high and glorious superlative faculty of knowledge, called Reason; the nature whereof is to admire him that is not only Life, Sense and Reason . . . but incomprehensibly greater. . . . All evil is unto the creature only, and cometh by excesse, and the improper use of things . . . as doth all good by the moderate and proper use of things. . . . Whatsoever is of Reason is above Sense, and seeketh not itself but in each others good, and would do it also. . . . This plain thing is that high thing spoken of by Christ, that would produce a new heaven and a new earth, wherein righteousness dwels, . . . that which shall produce the personall reigne of Christ. . . . When through Reason, by Faith in the practice of his Graces we have subdued the senses unto this frame we are . . . risen with him . . . to newnesse of life; not only here but shall by a change unto everlasting. This is that freedom where with he hath made us free. . . . All the slavery in the Christian world hath come by the sword, and mysterious Cheat of the heads of the Schools (vented in the Pulpits) by combining with the Anti-Christian policies of the ambitious Rulers thereof. For Christ, rightly preached, bringeth nothing but externall as well as internall freedom and peace."[11]

This confession of faith is interesting for several reasons. It confirms the close connection between the idea of reason and the Christian faith; it includes millenarian hopes, as well as a strong suspicion of rulers and clergymen; and it adds a new note by insisting on the conflict between the "slavery of the sword"

and Christian peace. This incipient pacifism of the disillusioned
soldier is highly characteristic of Jubbes' thought. During the
Putney debates he said: "Truly I do not know how to distinguish whether the spirit of God lives in me or no, but by
mercy, love, and peace; and on the contrary whether the spirit
of Antichrist lives in me, but by envy, malice, and war." Oliver
Cromwell seems to oave been aware of the implications of this
attitude. He commended Jubbes for the first part of his statement, but attacked the second part which he interpreted as
condemning the use of force, and he argued that "he that would
decline the doing of justice where there is no place for mercy,
and the exercise of the ways of force . . . doth . . . lead us
from that which is the law of the Spirit of Life."[12]

Jubbes, on the other hand, became more and more convinced that it was only "barbarous slavery which the Sword
doth ever usher in (though under the highest pretences of
Liberty),"[13] that the new rulers, the leaders of the Army,
might prove as evil as the King, and that it would therefore be
"more safe to have to do with a musled Lion, than a tame
serpent."[14] It was this conviction that was behind Jubbes'
proposals for a settlement, and not, by any means, partiality to
the King, for he believed with many Puritans that "Kings'
Courts are the fountains from whence the streames of excesse
doe flow, and that Kings are the Beasts spoken of in the
Revelation of John that thereby devoure the people, . . . exalting
with the horn of honour the covetous, the Extortioner, the
Damner, Swearer, Whorer, Gamester, Cheater, Liar and
lascivious Prodigalls."[15] In spite of this, he thought that the
lion could be so effectively muzzled, in the circumstances then
prevailing, that the liberties of the people and the privileges
of Englishmen could be securely established.

Among these liberties and "just things" he included "that
henceforth no Free-born person of this Nation be hereafter
pressed to serve in the Wars, that a generall revisement shall
be had of all the Lawes and Statutes now in force; that some
provisions be speedily made . . . for a conscientious and sufficient Reliefe for all the Poore and indigent People that none
may perish with want; that the common pastures . . . shall be
improved, and divided . . . as followeth, viz: One fourth part
whereof to the severall Tenants of the severall Parishes . . .
and one other fourth part to the poor of the same, and the other
two parts for the payment of the Souldiers; that all inslaving
tenures upon Record, by Oathes of fealty, Villanage, Homage

and fines at will of the Lords may all be bought in at such rates, as shall not exceed twenty years purchase to the Lord."[16] Jubbes also proposed the abolition of excise, the sale of Dean and Chapter lands, the settlement of Ireland ("that the Irish shall not still be proceeded against as to execute Cruelty for crueltie"), a redistribution of tithes to all "Teachers in the Word," and complete liberty of conscience including even Roman Catholics (the way of instructing the people in religion being referred to the Parliament).[17]

This programme was very similar to that of the Levellers. The social conception behind it was similar to William Walwyn's, for Jubbes wanted to see political power in the hands of "the most spotless man, as to excess, especially touching ambition and covetousness (the cause of our miseries) . . . that are or shall not be Ministers, late or present Members of this Parliament, Lawyers nor any Lords of Manners, or other person worth [more] than 500 pounds at the [most]."[18] Yet Jubbes never actually became a member of the Leveller group; he said on this point: "I am not a Leveller . . . or am of those gentlemens Councel's that were lately committed, [i.e. Lilburne, Walwyn, Overton, and Prince] (nor know I the cause thereof, for that I never read their book)."[19] Why this should have been so we do not know for certain; it may have had something to do with Jubbes' leaning towards pacifism, for he wrote: "When I left the Army, I found that I could not close with any single interest in England, but that I should . . . earnestly contend for Peace."[20]

We have seen that John Jubbes had come under the influence of certain religious currents and of many Leveller ideas on social and political questions. Although Jubbes showed uncommon force of character in laying down his commission in 1648, he was by no means an original thinker or an outstanding man, but his very mediocrity may be of value to us in showing that these two trends of thought were inextricably connected at that time. There were probably many who shared his thoughts but did not write them down. We are fortunate in Jubbes' case in being able to see the workings of an ordinary, slow-moving and deeply honest mind, and its awkward but determined attempts at expressing itself. His pacifism provides an interesting link with the convictions of the early Quakers. After the violent death of the King, Jubbes, with so many others, had "expected Righteousness, and immediately beheld as great iniquity and injustice as before," and so he probably came more than ever to believe that "in this . . . only resteth, and wholly dependeth, our Freedom; viz. to endeavour and obtain the avoiding of all force and Warres."[21]

NOTES TO APPENDIX B

[1] Anon., *Several Proposals*, x, ix, iv, ii. It is difficult to see why S. R. Gardiner should have thought that "there was too little practical knowledge of the world in this scheme to secure its acceptance" (*Civil War*, iv, 281).

[2] Cf. Gough, *History*, Jan. 1931, p. 337.

[3] Jubbes, *Apology*, p. 3. The pamphlet bears the date 4th May 1649 in the Thomason Collection.

[4] William Jubbes of Wymondham (granted arms in 1664 and died in 1680) had a brother John: cf. *The Visitation of Norfolk* (1664) (ed. A. W. Hughes Clarke and Arthur Campling, 1933), p. 113.

[5] C. H. Firth and G. Davies, *Regimental History of Cromwell's Army* (1940), p. 406.

[6] Jubbes, *Apology*, pp. 2, 7.

[7] Cf. *The Humble Remonstrance and Desires of Divers Officers and Souldiers . . . under Command of Colonel Hewson*, 4th Nov. 1647.

[8] Woodhouse, *Puritanism and Liberty*, pp. 99, 100.

[9] Jubbes, *Apology*, pp. 2, 19.

[10] Ibid., p. 17.

[11] Ibid., pp. 17, 18, 19.

[12] Woodhouse, op. cit., pp. 99, 106.

[13] Jubbes, *Apology*, p. 2.

[14] Jubbes, *Plea for Moderation*, pp. 2, 6. "A plea for Moderation in the Transactions of the Army, or, Weighty Observations upon the late Proposals for Peace, presented by the Honourable City of London, to Commissary General Ireton, for Concurrence of the Generall Councell. Humbly offered unto the consideration of the Officers of the Army; by Veritie Victor, Gent." (Thomason: 28th Dec. 1648) was almost certainly written by Jubbes. It was warmly recommended in Jubbes' Apology and is written in the same long-winded and cumbersome style, reiterating Jubbes' programme point by point.

He may have chosen the pseudonym in order to create the impression that his plan was being supported; his signature would not have carried much weight, as the officers knew that he was the author of the City Agreement.

[15] Jubbes, *Plea for Moderation*.

[16] Jubbes, *Apology*, pp. 16, 10, 12, 13.

[17] Ibid., pp. 12, 16, 13. In *Several Proposals* the public instruction is referred to the Ministry. This is one of only three relevant differences between that document and Jubbes' version of it. The two others are: (1) that Jubbes would have given the vote to persons worth £40 of personal estate instead of £50, and (2) that he would have included William Walwyn in the first "Committee of State."

[18] Ibid., p. 24. (Instead of [more] and [most] the text has [less] and [least], which is obviously a mistake.)

[19] Ibid., p. 7.

[20] Ibid., p. 1.

[21] Ibid., p. 5; *Plea for Moderation*, p. 5.

INDEX

178